VAN BUR
DECATUR,
P9-DFD-011

DISCARDED

101 Dog Tricks:
Kids Edition

You're good at walking on a leash, Jadie.

Thanks, so are you!

Can we slow down?

William Potter   Kyra   Jadie

101 Dog Tricks:
Kids Edition

Fun & Easy Activities, Games, and Crafts

Kyra Sundance

Quarry Books
100 Cummings Center, Suite 406L
Beverly, MA 01915

quarrybooks.com • craftside.typepad.com

7/14
Bkr

636.708
Sun

© 2014 Quarry Books
Text © 2014 by Kyra Sundance

First published in the United States of America in 2014 by
Quarry Books, a member of
Quarto Publishing Group USA Inc.
100 Cummings Center
Suite 406-L
Beverly, Massachusetts 01915-6101
Telephone: (978) 282-9590
Fax: (978) 283-2742
www.quarrybooks.com

All rights reserved. No part of this book may be reproduced in
any form without written permission of the copyright owners.
All images in this book have been reproduced with the
knowledge and prior consent of the artists concerned, and no
responsibility is accepted by the producer, publisher, or printer
for any infringement of copyright or otherwise, arising from the
contents of this publication. Every effort has been made to
ensure that credits accurately comply with information supplied.
We apologize for any inaccuracies that may have occurred and
will resolve inaccurate or missing information in a subsequent
reprinting of the book.

10 9 8 7 6 5 4 3 2 1

ISBN: 978-1-59253-893-5

Digital edition published in 2014
eISBN: 978-1-62788-029-9

Library of Congress Cataloging-in-Publication Data available

Design: Sundance Media (sundancemedia.com)
"Do More With Your Dog!" is a registered trademark of
    Kyra Sundance (domorewithyourdog.com)
Photography: Christian Arias, Slickforce Studios (slickforce.com)

Due to differing conditions, materials, and skill levels, the
publisher and various manufacturers disclaim any liability for
unsatisfactory results or injury due to improper use of
tools, materials, or information.

Printed in China

DoMoreWithYourDog.com

CONTENTS

5 FOR THE ATHLETES

6 BRAIN GAMES

7 AMAZING ART

8 USEFUL THINGS

For Kids Only

Things you need:
1. treats
2. a dog
3. this book

Hold the treat between your fingers like this . . .

BEST treats . . .
1. hot dogs
2. ham
3. steak
4. chicken
5. cheese
6. goldfish crackers
7. cheese puffs
8. pizza crusts

Do more with your dog!

Like this . . .

. . . so your fingers won't get nipped

* this is not a wolf

Not like this

Before using
this book

Ta da!

After using
this book

⭐ Best TIPS . . .

1. Keep lessons short
2. Train happy
3. Don't say "no!"
4. Don't make it too hard too fast
5. Give the treat the instant your dog does it
6. Always end on a success, with your dog happy
7. If it's not working, use ham

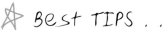

Why kids are better dog trainers than adults

1. Kids follow directions
2. they don't yell at their dog
3. they give lots of treats
4. they make training fun
5. Kids are short (and so are dogs)

Hi. This is me. Kyra.

world-famous dog trainer

Jadie (world famous dog)

♡ ♡
♡

Likes ham →

* If your dog acts like this, read page 96

Bobbing for Popcorn

BEFORE YOU START

Does your dog like popcorn? If not, use cheese puffs, goldfish crackers, or Cheerios.

TROUBLESHOOTING

MY DOG WON'T GO IN THE WATER

Some dogs love water and some do not. Never lift your dog into the pool; let him decide on his own when he is ready to enter.

TEACH IT:

This is a great game to play with your dog on a hot summer day. Teach him to become comfortable in water by having him to pick out popcorn from a shallow pool. Go ahead, dive right in!

1. Sit in an empty, dry wading pool and hold out some popcorn to your dog. He will be unsure about the wading pool and will need a little time to get used to it before he is confident enough to step inside.

2. Put just an inch (2 cm) of water in the pool. Move your treat across to the middle of the pool to try to get your dog to follow it and step inside.

3. Put a little more water in the pool. Toss some popcorn in the water. Your dog will try to get the popcorn, but may be hesitant to step all the way inside. That's okay, give him time to get used to it.

4. Fill the pool to the top. Sprinkle popcorn in the pool and let your dog have fun finding them and fishing them out.

WHAT TO EXPECT: Some dogs adore water and will splash right in. Other dogs will act like they don't want to get their paws wet at all! Be patient with your dog and he'll become more brave.

1 Sit in an empty pool. Offer your dog popcorn. He might be a little scared of the pool at first.

2 Put a little water in the pool. Move a treat over to the middle of the pool to try to get your dog to step inside.

3 Put a little water in the pool and toss in some popcorn. Your dog will be hesitant at first.

4 Fill the pool to the top. Sprinkle in several popcorn pieces and let your dog find them and fish them out.

Muffin Tin

BEFORE YOU START
Small, hard treats work best for this game. You can even use your dog's kibble for treats.

TROUBLESHOOTING

MY DOG GIVES UP
Quickly lift one of the tennis balls to show your dog the treat underneath. That should motivate him to keep trying.

MY CRAZY DOG KNOCKS THE WHOLE THING OVER
Hold the edges of the muffin tin with your hands or stand up and hold it with your feet.

TIP! Visit a public tennis court and ask players if they'd like to donate old balls for your dog.

TEACH IT:

Hide tiny treats in a muffin tin and cover the cups with tennis balls. Can your dog figure out how to get the treats?

1. Let your dog watch as you place one treat in each muffin tin cup.
2. Tell your dog excitedly to "find it!" and let him come and eat the treats.
3. Try the same thing again, only this time place a tennis ball in one of the cups (on top of a treat). Encourage your dog to get all of the treats, including the one under the ball.
4. The next time, put treats in all the cups and cover half of them with tennis balls. Can your dog find all of the treats?
5. A real pro will be able to find the treats even with balls covering ALL of the cups!

WHAT TO EXPECT: Dogs love this game! With your encouragement your dog can learn this game in ten minutes.

1   Place a treat in each cup.

2   Encourage your dog to "find it!" and let him eat the treats.

3   This time, place a tennis ball over one of the treats. Can your dog move the ball to find the treat?

4   Hide half of the treats with tennis balls.

5   Give your dog a real challenge by placing balls on top of all of the cups.

Dog Bowling

BEFORE YOU START

If you don't have bowling pins, use empty plastic soda or water bottles.

TROUBLESHOOTING

MY DOG RUNS AROUND THE PINS AND NOT OVER THEM

Set up barriers such as large boxes on the sides of the pins.

MY DOG JUMPS OVER THE PINS

Your dog is athletic. Spread the pins out more, or add more pins. When you show him the treat and call him, hold the treat close to the ground and not up high.

TIP! Allowing dogs to play with new things will make them more confident.

TEACH IT:

Call your dog through a narrow lane of bowling pins, and see who can get him to knock over the most pins. Strike!

1. Set up bowling pins in a narrow hallway, with one person at either end of the hall.

2. Call your dog to you. It may help to have a treat in your hand when you call him. When he runs to you he will crash through the bowling pins.

3. Give your dog the treat and count how many pins he knocked over. Reset the pins and have the other person call him this time. How many pins did he knock over this time? Did he beat his record?

WHAT TO EXPECT: Big, goofy dogs are often good at this game and crash right through the pins. Smaller dogs are more worried about getting hurt and try to run between the pins. With a little practice, your dog will get the hang of it in no time.

1 Set up bowling pins in a narrow hallway, with one person at either end.

2 Call your dog to you (it may help to show him a treat in your hand). He will crash through the pins.

3 Give your dog the treat and count how many pins he knocked over. Did he beat his record?

Memory Game

BEFORE YOU START
You'll need three pails, or bowls, or dog food bowls.

TROUBLESHOOTING

MY DOG IS JUST GUESSING
When learning, often dogs will go to the last pail that produced a treat. So if *last* time he found a treat in the red pail, he'll go straight to the red pail again (even though he just saw you put a treat in the blue pail!). It's a dog thing. Keep practicing.

TIP! Make it easier for your dog by moving the pails farther apart from each other.

TEACH IT:
Hmmm . . . now which one had the treat?

1. Set out two identical pails a few feet apart. Tell your dog to **stay** (page 189) or have someone hold his collar.

2. Show your dog as you put a treat into one pail.

3. Tell him to "find it!" If he goes to the correct pail, he gets to eat the treat! If he goes first to the wrong pail, don't allow him to then check the other pail as well. Instead, put him back in a sit-stay and start all over.

4. Ready to make it harder? Try *three* pails! This will be a lot harder for your dog.

WHAT TO EXPECT: This game is surprisingly difficult for dogs but is excellent training for their focus and memory. Even when your dog has mastered the two-pail game, he will find it quite difficult to be successful with three pails.

1　Set out two pails. Tell your dog to stay.

2　Show your dog as you put a treat into one pail.

3　Say "find it!" If he goes to the correct pail he gets to eat the treat. If not, he gets nothing.

4　Make it harder with three pails.

Follow the Bread Crumb Trail

BEFORE YOU START

Use rather large treats that your dog can see. Popcorn works well if your dog likes that treat.

TROUBLESHOOTING

MY DOG CAN'T FIND THE PATH OF TREATS

Put the treats closer together. Also try using smellier treats (liver and salmon treats are pretty smelly).

TEACH IT:

Drop a trail of treats through your yard. Can your dog follow the path and find the treasure at the end?

1. Lay a line of treats through your yard, or down a path. Put them a few feet apart. Put a treasure at the end, like a special dog bone or toy.

2. Leash your dog and show him the first treat. Let him sniff out the path. As he starts to find more treats he'll get more excited and pull you along. Did he find the treasure at the end?

WHAT TO EXPECT: This is a fun and simple game for any dog. Some dogs can get quite excited to find the treats and will pull on their leash.

1. Lay down a line of treats through your yard.

2. Put your dog on a leash and let him follow the trail.

Laundry Basket

TEACH IT:

Does your dog have a favorite toy? Or does he prefer food treats? Hide his favorite thing under a laundry basket. He can see the toy, and smell the toy, but can't get the toy. Oh no, will he figure out this puzzle?

1. Show your dog as you put his favorite bone or toy under a laundry basket. Let him poke around at it for ten seconds, and then tilt it up so he can squeeze under and get his toy. Now we've got him interested in this game!

2. Try the game again, only this time let your dog try it by himself a little longer before you help him. He's got to learn to figure it out on his own.

BEFORE YOU START
Food toys work well with this game. Try a peanut butter–filled toy or a chewable bone.

TROUBLESHOOTING

MY DOG GIVES UP RIGHT AWAY
Make sure you've got something he really wants under the laundry basket (usually food!). Try this game on grass, as the laundry basket will tip over on grass instead of sliding on carpet.

TIP! Put a dog food bowl with some food in it under the laundry basket.

1. Hide your dog's toy under a laundry basket. After ten seconds, tilt it up.

2. Let your dog struggle with it on his own. Can he figure out how to get it?

Roll Out the Carpet

BEFORE YOU START
A hallway rug works great for this game, but you can also use a blanket or a towel.

TIP! Use treats that have a lot of smell, such as liver treats, salmon treats, or pieces of beef jerky.

TEACH IT:

Teach your dog to roll out the carpet. Hide treats inside the roll, and your dog will find one with every push.

1. Get a handful of small treats. Lay them in a line down the whole length of your rug.
2. Roll up the rug with the treats inside.
3. Point out the first treat to your dog. As he nudges his nose to get the treat, the rug will unroll a little bit. As he sniffs and eats more treats, the rug will continue to unroll.

WHAT TO EXPECT: This is an easy game that any dog can learn. In the beginning put lots of treats inside the rug, but as your dog gets better you can put fewer treats in there, or even just one big treat at the end.

1. Lay a line of treats down the center of a rug.

2. Roll it up with the treats inside.

3. As your dog sniffs at each treat, the rug will unroll.

Search in Ball Pit

TEACH IT:

Even dogs think it's fun to jump in a ball pit! Hide a treat or toy in a bucket full of balls and watch your dog dive in after it.

1 You'll need a smelly food toy like a chewable bone, a peanut butter–filled toy, or even a baggie filled with treats. Show your dog the bone to get her interest, and lay it right on top of the balls. Tell her to "get it!"

2 When she finds the bone, let her play with it for a while as a reward.

3 Bury the bone a little deeper (but not too deep).

4 Your dog will have to hunt for it this time. Where did it go? Can she find it?

WHAT TO EXPECT: Some dogs are cautious about putting their head under all of those balls, but they usually gain confidence over time. Don't make it too hard for your dog too fast. Bury the bone just a little deeper each time.

BEFORE YOU START
Instead of balls, you can also use crumpled newspaper balls in a large box.

1 Lay the bone right on top of the balls.

2 Let her have the bone as a reward.

3 Bury the bone a little deeper.

4 Your dog will have to hunt for it this time. Can she find it?

Find Hidden Treats

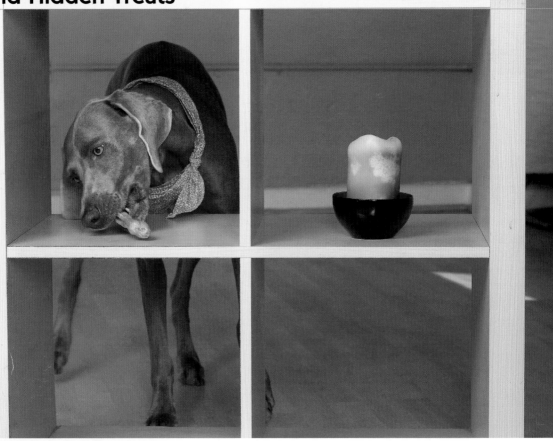

BEFORE YOU START
Use small treats like dog kibble, goldfish crackers, popcorn, cheese puffs, or Cherrios cereal.

TROUBLESHOOTING
MY DOG CAN'T FIND THE TREATS
Use smellier treats like pieces of cheese, hot dog, or beef jerky.

TIP! Count how many treats you hide. When your dog has finished searching, check each spot to make sure she got them all. You don't want mom to step on one later!

TEACH IT:
Hide treats around the house and watch your dog sleuth them out. Bet she can find them all!

1. Tell your dog to "stay." If she doesn't know that word, then have someone hold her collar.
2. Hide a treat in a really easy spot, just a few feet away from her, on or near the floor.
3. Say "find it!" and point to the treat.
4. Try it again, but this time hide the treat in a little harder spot, like up off the floor. Don't make it too hard yet though.
5. As your dog improves, you can hide the treats under cushions, behind doors, or even in other rooms. Have your dog wait while you run around the house and hide a whole bunch of treats.

WHAT TO EXPECT: Most dogs learn this game really easily and will keep busy searching for treats for ten minutes at a time.

1 Tell your dog to "stay," or have someone hold her collar.

2 Hide a treat a few feet away near the floor.

3 Say "find it!" and point to the treat.

4 Try again, but hide the treat in a harder spot.

5 Later you can hide a whole bunch of treats all over the house.

Untie the Knot

BEFORE YOU START
If your dog has ever tried to rip or eat towels, then this is not a good game for her.

TIP! Tie the knot loosely to make it easier for your dog.

TEACH IT:
Can a dog untie a knot? Why not!

1. Find an old towel or dish towel. You might want to cut it in half lengthwise so it is not too wide. Lay some treats on the towel and tie it in a knot. Cram some additional treats into the knot so that they are partially sticking out.

2. Give the towel to your dog and let her work at the knot until she gets it untied.

WHAT TO EXPECT: Dogs are usually a little timid the first few times you show them this game but they will get more excited about it every time they play it. Don't make it too hard for your dog at first.

1. Lay some treats on the towel and tie it in a knot.

2. Give the knotted towel to your dog, and let her figure out how to work the knot out.

Backtrack to Your Toy

TEACH IT:

How good is your dog's memory? Challenge him to remember the location of his toy, and then go back to find it.

1. Show your dog his favorite toy (or food toy, or bowl with food in it) and set it on the ground. Point it out to him a few times and tell him to remember where it is.

2. Use a leash to walk him a short distance (about 30 feet, 10 meters) away from the toy.

3. Excitedly say, "Find it!" and maybe even point toward the toy. Let your dog run back to the toy or food bowl and get his reward. Next, place the toy in a new location and walk your dog farther away from the toy and try again.

WHAT TO EXPECT: Build distance gradually so your dog can be successful and won't get discouraged. Eventually you may be able to backtrack a few hundred feet.

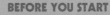

BEFORE YOU START
This is an outdoor game, for a place with plenty of room.

1. Put his toy on the ground and tell him to remember where it is.

2. Walk him about 30 feet (10 meters) away.

3. Tell your dog to "find it!" and let him run back to the toy.

Messenger Dog

BEFORE YOU START

For this game you'll need two people and one top-secret message.

TROUBLESHOOTING

MY DOG WON'T LEAVE ME BECAUSE HE KNOWS I HAVE TREATS IN MY POCKET

The first time is the hardest, and then your dog will figure out that you both have treats. Start close together so the other person can hold out her treat toward your dog.

TIP! Use each of your family members' names. Over time your dog will learn who is who.

TEACH IT:

In this game your dog carries a top-secret message back and forth between two people, just like historic war dogs did.

1. Attach a top-secret message to your dog's collar using a messenger collar pouch (page 28). Each person should have a pocketful of yummy treats. Separate a short distance, and have one person call the dog.

2. As the dog approaches, clap your hands and encourage him. When he arrives, say "good boy!" and give him a treat.

3. Send the dog to the other person by saying, "Find Taylor!" (If the other person's name isn't Taylor, then use his or her name instead.) When the dog gets to him or her, the other person gives the dog a treat.

4. Now make it more difficult, by running away and disappearing around a corner. Can your dog still find you? After you've sent your dog, take that time to hide yourself in a new spot. Keep the game going, sending your dog back and forth between people.

WHAT TO EXPECT: Dogs enjoy this game because they get a treat with each delivery (don't forget the treats!). Send notes back and forth to your friend with this special delivery.

1 Start a short distance apart. Call your dog enthusiastically.

2 Give your dog a treat when he gets to you.

Make a messenger collar pouch from dad's old shirt (page 28).

3 Send him back to your sister for another treat.

4 Make it more difficult by running around a corner. Can he find you this time?

Make a Messenger Dog Collar Pouch

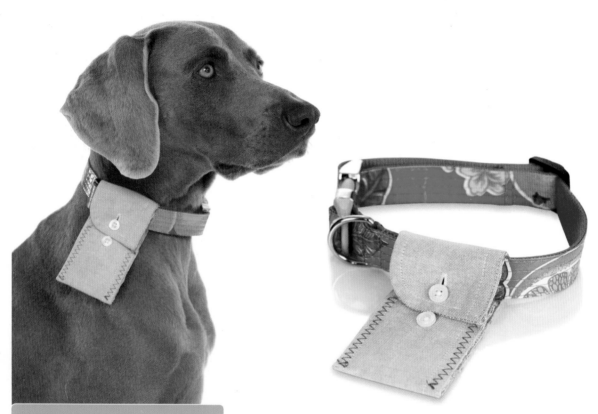

SUPPLIES
- Dad's button-down shirt
- Needle and thread

TROUBLESHOOTING

I DON'T KNOW HOW TO SEW

It's easy! Thread the needle and tie the two ends of your thread together. Poke the needle up and down along the shirt cuff. At the end, poke your needle through the same spot a few times to secure it.

TIP! Pick up inexpensive button-down shirts at the thrift store.

MAKE IT:

Make this collar pouch so that your dog can deliver your secret messages. Teach her how to deliver messages by using the instructions on page 26.

1 Get one of dad's old shirts that has a buttoned cuff on the sleeve.

2 Cut off one of the cuffs. (Who needs cuffs, anyway?)

3 The cuff has buttons on one end and a buttonhole on the other.

4 Fold the cuff into thirds, with the buttons on the outside. Use a needle and thread to stitch the sides.

5 Now it's ready to hold your secret message! Fold it over your dog's collar and button it to secure it.

FINISHING TOUCHES: Use this pouch to deliver secret messages, or just to hold some items for your dog, like a treat or pickup bags.

1. Get one of dad's old shirts.

2. Cut off the cuff on the sleeve.

3. The cuff has buttons and a buttonhole.

4. Stitch up both sides.

5. Put in your secret message.

Teach your dog to deliver messages (page 26).

Dig in the Sand Pit

BEFORE YOU START

Instead of sand, you can use a basin filled with rubber mulch pieces (as in this photo).

TROUBLESHOOTING

MY DOG WON'T DIG

Dogs will dig for food. Put some strong-smelling food (like hot dogs) in a sandwich bag and bury that. Yes, your dog can smell right through the bag!

TEACH IT:

Dogs love to dig. Bury a treasure and have your dog dig it out . . . just don't bury it in mom's rose garden (oops!).

1. Some dogs have a favorite toy that they are crazy about, like a tennis ball. Other dogs prefer food toys. Bury your dog's favorite toy so it is sticking halfway out of the sand. Point to it and encourage your dog to "get it!" Dig a little yourself to show your dog what to do.

2. When your dog finds her toy, let her have it as a reward.

WHAT TO EXPECT: Once your dog gets the hang of it, bury the toy deeper under the sand. Dogs can get excited and send sand flying everywhere!

1. Bury your dog's favorite toy so it is showing a little above the sand. Encourage her to "get it!"

2. Let her play with the toy once she uncovers it.

Toy Under a Blanket

TEACH IT:

Now you see it . . . now you don't. Where did your toy go?

1 Some dogs like plush toys and some like food-filled toys. Use whichever toy or bone that your dog loves. Show your dog as you put the toy on top of a blanket. Tell her to "get it!" and let her play with the toy as a reward.

2 Let your dog watch as you partially cover the toy with a blanket. Can she find the toy this time? Can she get it from beneath the blanket?

WHAT TO EXPECT: It's harder than you'd think for a dog to get her toy out from under a blanket. If your dog struggles with it, help her sort out the blanket a bit. She'll get the hang of it soon.

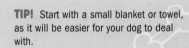

TIP! Start with a small blanket or towel, as it will be easier for your dog to deal with.

1 Put your dog's favorite toy on top of a blanket. Tell her to "get it!"

2 Partially cover it with a blanket and let your dog uncover it. Later, cover it up completely.

Hide-and-Seek

BEFORE YOU START

It will come in handy to first teach your dog to **stay** (page 189).

TROUBLESHOOTING

MY DOG FINDS ME TOO FAST

Your dog is finding you by smell (they have awesome noses!). Here's how to make it harder for him: walk into several different rooms before going to your hiding spot. Your dog will smell every room that you went in to and will have to check them all.

TIP! Instead of saying "find me," use your name: "find Daisy." That way your dog will start to learn your name.

TEACH IT:

Bored? No friends to play with? How about a game of hide-and-seek with your dog!

1   Put some treats in your pocket. Tell your dog to "stay." (If your dog doesn't know how to stay, have another person hold his collar.) Hide just a few feet away from your dog, behind the sofa.

2   Call to your dog to "find me!" When your dog finds you, give him a treat.

3   Try the game again, but this time hide just outside of the room. Call to your dog to "find me!"

4   Always reward your dog for finding you. That's what makes the game fun for him!

WHAT TO EXPECT: Dogs love this game (and so do kids!). As your dog improves, choose harder and harder hiding places like in the closet, under the bed, or behind a door. If your dog has trouble finding you, make a little noise to help him.

1 Tell your dog to "stay" or have someone hold his collar. Hide behind the sofa.

2 Call to your dog to "find me!" Reward him with a treat.

3 Now try hiding just outside the room.

4 It's important to give your dog a treat every time he finds you.

easy

Soccer Ball Roll

BEFORE YOU START

Play this game on carpet, so the bowl doesn't slide across the floor.

TROUBLESHOOTING

MY DOG WON'T PUSH THE BALL OUT OF THE BOWL

Some dogs don't like to be pushy. Try a lightweight inflatable ball instead, which will move with the slightest push from your dog.

TIP! This can be a fun way to feed your dog her dinner, one kibble at a time!

TEACH IT:

Sports star dogs will get a kick out of this game, as they learn how to roll a soccer ball. Score!

1 Show your dog as you drop a treat into her food bowl.

2 Place a soccer ball on top of the treat. If your dog is hesitant, roll the ball off the treat for a second to show her that the treat is still under there.

3 Give her a chance to figure out how to move the ball. She may use her nose or her paw.

4 When your dog finally gets the soccer ball out of the bowl, let her eat the treat as a reward.

5 It won't take long at all before she is a pro at pushing the soccer ball. Score!

WHAT TO EXPECT: Dogs usually pick up this game within ten minutes.

1 Drop a treat into your dog's food bowl.

2 Place a soccer ball on top of the treat.

3 Let her figure out how to move the ball.

4 When your dog rolls the ball out of the bowl, let her have the treat.

5 Soon she'll learn how to roll the ball off the bowl.

Kibble Run

MAKE IT:

Plink, plink, plunk . . . there goes the kibble, rolling down your ladder of tubes. Will it make it all the way down to your dog?

1. Cover paper towel tubes in colorful duct tape.

2. Cut off squares from both ends of the tube. These openings will catch the kibble as it falls down.

3. Glue magnets to the ends of the tube, right on edge of the opening that you cut.

4. Using the magnets, stick the tubes on your refrigerator. Arrange the tubes in a zigzag pattern.

PLAY THE KIBBLE RUN GAME: Drop a dog food kibble in the top tube and watch it fall through all the tubes. You may have to play with it a bit until you get it just right. If the kibble makes it to the floor, your dog gets to eat it.

SUPPLIES
- Paper towel tubes
- Duct tape
- Glue
- Small magnets

TIP! If mom won't let you build your kibble run on the refrigerator, attach metal cookie pans to the wall and stick your magnet tubes on them.

STEPS:

1 Cover the paper towel tubes with colorful duct tape.

2 Cut off squares from both ends of the tube.

3 Glue a magnet near the cut edge.

Glue another magnet on the other side.

4 Use the magnets to arrange the tubes in a zigzag shape.

No-Sew Dog Bed

SUPPLIES
- Fleece fabric
- Marker and ruler
- Cotton batting

TROUBLESHOOTING

MY STRIPS DON'T MATCH UP; I HAVE ONE EXTRA

That's okay, simply tie your leftover strip to another pair of strips.

TIP! Instead of cotton batting, you can stuff your bed with old T-shirts or pillows.

MAKE IT:

This easy dog bed takes just a few hours to make, and makes a great gift. Even little kids can do it!

1. Cut two same-sized rectangles of fleece fabric. Fleece does not fray.

2. Use a marker and ruler to make dots every 1½ inches (4 cm) around all four edges of your fabric. Do this to both of your fleece squares. You don't need to be super exact with this. If you don't want to use a ruler, you can just do it by eye.

3. At every dot, make a cut about 3 inches (8 cm) deep. Don't worry, it doesn't have to be exact. When you get to the corner, you will end up cutting out a square piece.

4. Lay your two squares on top of each other. Starting at one corner, tie two strips together. Work your way around the entire bed.

5. Oops! Don't forget to leave an opening for the stuffing! Stuff in cotton batting and then tie the opening shut.

FINISHING TOUCHES: Finished! You've got a great gift for your dog or for someone else's dog. Make an extra bed to donate to the animal shelter. Sweet!

1 Cut two same-sized rectangles of fleece.

2 Make dots every 1½ inches (4 cm) around the edges of your fabric.

3 Cut about 3 inches deep (8 cm) at every dot. At the corner you will cut out a piece.

4 Lay your fleece squares on top of each other. Starting at the corner, tie the strips together.

5 Before you finish tying the last strips, leave an opening for the stuffing.

Ta-dah! A handmade dog bed!

Roly-Poly Treat Roller Toy

SUPPLIES
- Cardboard oatmeal canister
- Paper towel holder (wall mounted)

TROUBLESHOOTING

MY DOG PUSHES THE WHOLE CANISTER UP AND OFF OF THE DISPENSER
Put some tape across the dispenser brackets so that the rod cannot be pushed out of the slots.

TIP! Making the holes takes a bit of work. Puncture a small hole, and then use closed scissors or your fingers to widen the hole.

MAKE IT:

This tumbling toy has holes that drop out treats as your dog spins it. What fun!

1. Remove the lid from your oatmeal canister and cut a hole in its center. The hole should be about the size of a paper towel tube.

2. Turn the canister upside down and cut a similar hole in the bottom.

3. Now make a bunch of holes in the canister. Make the holes big enough for dog kibble to fit through.

4. Pour some dog food kibble into the canister and replace the lid.

5. Feed the paper towel dispenser rod through the canister so it hangs just like a roll of paper towels. Mount it on your wall, at dog height.

GET YOUR DOG STARTED: Show your dog how to use this toy by rolling it a bit yourself. Once she sees treats falling out she'll become interested in it and start to nose it herself. In the beginning, put lots of kibble inside so even short rolls will make kibble fall out.

1. Cut a hole in the center of the lid that is about the size of a paper towel tube.

2. Cut a similarly sized hole in the bottom of the canister.

3. Make a bunch of smaller holes all over the canister.

4. Pour in some dog kibble.

5. Hang the canister just like you would hang a roll of paper towels.

Polka Dog Treat Pot

SUPPLIES
- Paint
- 6–inch (15 cm) flower pot
- 6–inch (15 cm) saucer
- Round stickers
- Tape
- 2–inch (5 cm) wood ball knob
- Glue

TIP! Almost any kind of paint can be used on ceramic, but spray paint will give the nicest smooth finish.

MAKE IT:

Your dog is one-of-a-kind. He needs a one-of-a-kind cookie jar to hold his most valuable possessions . . . his treats!

1. Paint the inside and outside of your pot and saucer.
2. Put a piece of tape over the hole in the pot to keep treats from dropping out.
3. Stick round stickers all over the pot.
4. Wrap painter's tape or masking tape around the rim of the pot.
5. Turn the pot upside down and paint the whole outside of the pot (including the stickers and tape) with a different color of paint.
6. Peel off the stickers and tape to reveal the color below.
7. Paint the wood ball knob and glue it onto the saucer (super glue works best). Let it dry for 24 hours.

FINISHING TOUCHES: Write your dog's name on the container or decorate it with stickers or wood cutouts. Fill with treats!

1 Spray paint your pot and saucer.

2 Tape over the hole at the bottom of the pot.

3 Stick stickers all over the pot.

4 Wrap tape around the rim.

5 Paint the outside of the pot with a different color.

6 Peel off the stickers and tape.

7 Glue the wood ball knob to the saucer.

Duct Tape Treat Bag

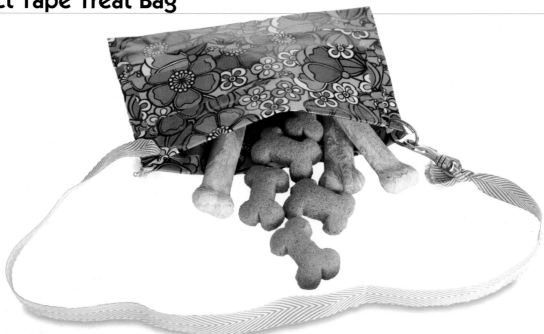

SUPPLIES
- Zipper-seal sandwich bag
- Duct tape
- O-ring
- Ribbon
- Bolt snap clip or other fastener

TIP! Wear your treat bag every time you train. When your dog sees you put it on she will get excited to train!

MAKE IT:

Every dog trainer needs a treat bag to hold treats. Make this stylish one in your choice of colors and patterns.

1. Lay your sandwich bag on the table. Starting at the end with the opening, lay a strip of duct tape across the bag. The strip of tape should go past the sides of the sandwich bag.

2. Continue laying more strips of tape until the whole side is covered.

3. Flip the sandwich bag over and fold in the end pieces.

4. Add short pieces of tape until this side is all covered with tape too.

5. The bottom of the treat bag is the weakest point, so add one more piece of tape there. Fold it so it covers the bottom of the bag. Trim off the ends with scissors.

6. With scissors, cut both side seams HALFWAY.

7. Fold the flaps inside the bag.

8. Punch a hole into each of the top corners. In one corner, attach your O-ring. In the other corner, fasten your ribbon with a knot.

9. Attach a bolt snap or fastener to the other end of your ribbon. Swing it around your waist and clip the fastener to the O-ring. Now you look like a pro!

FINISHING TOUCHES: Adjust the length of the ribbon to suit you. Wear it around your waist or over your shoulder and across your chest.

1 Starting at the end with the opening, lay a strip of tape across the bag.

2 Lay more strips until the whole side is covered.

3 Flip the sandwich bag over and fold in the end pieces.

4 Add short pieces of tape to finish this side.

5 Fold a piece of tape over the bottom for additional strength. Trim the ends.

(continued)

Duct Tape Treat Bag (continued)

6 Cut halfway down the side seams.

7 Fold the flaps inside the bag.

8 Punch a hole into the top corners. Attach the O-ring in one, and a ribbon in the other.

9 Attach a bolt snap to the ribbon and clip it to the O-ring.

easy

Soggy Dog Doormat

MAKE IT:

It's raining outside and your soggy dog tracked wet pawprints on mom's clean floors . . . oh no! Better make your wet pooch his own absorbent mat to wipe off on.

1. Turn a bath mat upside down. Use a marker to draw a large bone shape. If you make a mistake, that's okay, just draw a new line. This side of the mat won't show anyway.

2. Use a good pair of scissors to cut out your shape.

3. There will be lots of fluff on the edges where you cut out. Brush it all off now, so it doesn't come off in little pieces later.

SUPPLIES
- Bath mat
- Marker
- Scissors

TIP! Can you think of other shapes for your doormat? How about a dog house shape, or a heart?

1. Draw a bone shape on the bottom of the mat.

2. Cut out the bone.

3. Brush off the loose pieces around the edge.

easy

Pawprint Clay Ornament

SUPPLIES
- 2 cups (240 g) flour
- 1 cup (290 g) salt
- 1 cup (235 ml) lukewarm water
- Paint
- Ribbon

TIP! Mix some food coloring or colored chalk into your dough as an alternative to paint.

MAKE IT:

Make a lasting memory with this special holiday ornament. Hang it from the tree or give it as a gift.

1. Mix 2 cups (240 g) flour and 1 cup (290 g) salt in a bowl. Slowly add 1 cup (235 ml) lukewarm water. Knead it for several minutes until it is smooth and workable.

2. Roll out the dough onto a cookie sheet until it is about 1 inch (2 cm) thick.

3. Do the paw print. If your dog messes it up the first time (which she probably will), then roll out the dough and try again.

4. Cut a circle around the paw print by pressing a bowl on top of the dough. Pull off the dough that is outside the bowl. Use a pencil to make a hole on top of your ornament for the ribbon.

5. Pop it in a 200°F degree (100°C) oven for 3 hours. You can also just let it air-dry for a couple of days. Once it is completely hardened and cooled, paint it and add the ribbon.

FINISHING TOUCHES: Use a permanent marker to write your dog's name and the date on the back of the ornament. A coat of varnish will make it shine.

1 Mix salt and flour in a bowl and slowly add lukewarm water.

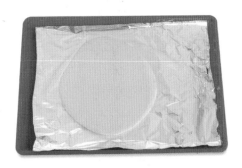

2 Roll out the dough until it is about 1 inch (2 cm) thick.

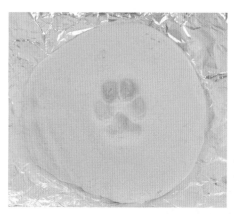

3 Put your dog's paw into the dough. Easier said than done!

4 Cut a circle around the paw print by using a bowl. Make a hole for the ribbon.

5 Let it air-dry or pop it in the oven. Once cooled, paint it and attach the ribbon.

easy

Fleece Leash

SUPPLIES
- Fleece fabric
- Bolt snap leash clip

TIP! Clip the bolt snap to something while you braid to keep the leash taut.

MAKE IT:

This comfy leash is soft on your hands and lightweight for your dog. Make it in under an hour!

1. Cut three strips of fleece fabric that are about 1½ to 2 inches wide (4 to 5 cm), and about 5 feet long (1½ m).

2. Pull the three strips through the leash clip and tie it off with a knot.

3. Braid the strips together.

4. When you reach the end of the strips, tie a knot right over the braided part and pull it tight. Don't worry if your ends are uneven.

5. Make the leash handle by poking the knot through the leash. It might be tough to push it through, but keep working at it.

6. Cut off the ends past the knot. That's it!

FINISHING TOUCHES: Use this same technique to make a matching belt for yourself. Or make a short braided rope as a tug toy for your dog.

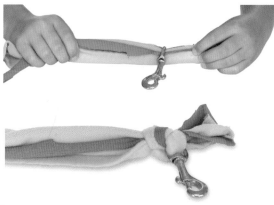

1. Cut three strips of fabric 1½ to 2 inches wide (4 to 5 cm) by 5 feet (1½ m) long.

2. Pull the three strips through the leash clip and tie it off with a knot.

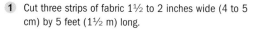

3. Braid the strips together.

4. When you reach the end, tie a knot over the braided part.

5. Make the leash handle by poking the knot through the leash.

6. Cut off the ends past the knot. Finished!

No-Sew Bandana

SUPPLIES
- Fabric
- Hem tape
- Iron

TROUBLESHOOTING

I'M HAVING TROUBLE FOLDING THE FABRIC OVER THE HEM TAPE

Does it keep unfolding on you? Try this: first fold the edge and iron it (without the hem tape). That will make a nice crease. Then when you put the hem tape down, the crease will help hold the edge in place.

TIP! Fabric stores sell pre-cut fabric "quilt squares" which are 18 by 21 inches (46 by 53 cm). These make nice bandanas. Your triangles won't be symmetrical, but that's okay.

MAKE IT:

Give your dog some style with a colorful bandana. Make one in every color to match your outfits. Sweet!

1. Cut a square of fabric: 21 by 21 inches (53 by 53 cm) is a good size for medium and large dogs, but you'll want a smaller square for the little guys.

2. Fold the two corners together to make a triangle. Cut along the fold so that you end up with two triangles.

3. Lay your fabric on an ironing board with the non-pretty side facing up. Lay a strip of hem tape along one entire side, about an inch (2.5 cm) from the edge. Fold the edge over it. Hem tape turns to glue when you heat it.

4. Set your steam iron to the "wool" (low) setting. Place a damp cloth over the bandana. Press the iron for 10 seconds on the bandana edge, and then move it to the next section. Do not slide the iron. Flip the bandana upside down and repeat on the other side. Allow to cool. If the bond is not secure, press again. Repeat this for all three sides of the bandana.

5. Clip off the funny corners. Now that's a professional-looking bandana!

FINISHING TOUCHES: Use fabric markers to write your dog's name. Sew on colorful buttons or glue blingy beads. Get creative! Make a matching bandana for yourself.

1. Cut a square of fabric 21 by 21 inches (53 by 53 cm).

2. Fold the corners together into a triangle. Cut along the fold.

3. Lay hem tape 1 inch (2.5 cm) from the edge. Fold the fabric over the hem tape.

4. Cover with a damp cloth and press the iron down for 10 seconds on each side.

5. Clip off the funny corners.

Scented Calming Collar

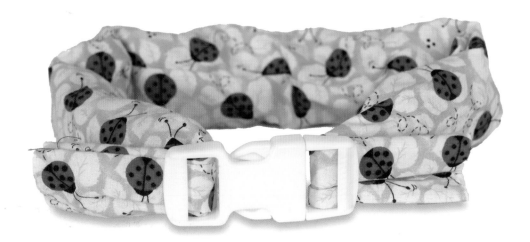

SUPPLIES
- Fabric
- Needle and thread
- Collar buckle
- Scented filling such as potpourri, rose petals, scented beads, herbal tea, or rice mixed with vanilla or scented oil

TIP! Lavender has been shown to be a particularly effective calming scent.

MAKE IT:

Is your dog hyper? Soothe her nerves with a collar scented with relaxing lavender, vanilla, or rose petals. Clip this collar on your dog and let the fragrance work naturally to calm her.

1 Cut a strip of fabric 4 inches wide by about 21 inches long (10 by 53 cm). If your dog has a really big neck, you may need to make it longer.

2 Fold the fabric in half lengthwise, with the pretty side on the inside. Stitch the entire length of it (but leave both ends open).

3 Turn it inside out so the pretty side is now on the outside.

4 Feed one end through the buckle.

5 Fill the open end with rose petals or other scented filling.

6 When it is full of rose petals, poke the open end of the fabric through the other side of the buckle. Put it on your dog.

FINISHING TOUCHES: Adjust the length by pulling it tighter through the buckle. Leave a couple of inches (5 to 7 cm) on either end to hold it secure, and snip off any extra fabric.

1 Cut a strip of fabric 4 inches wide by 21 inches long (10 by 53 cm).

2 Fold the fabric in half with the pretty side inside. Stitch the length of it (but leave both ends open)

3 Turn it inside out.

4 Feed one end through the buckle.

5 Fill the open end with rose petals.

6 Feed the open end through the other side of the buckle. Put it on your dog.

Crinkle Dog Toy

SUPPLIES
- Water bottle
- Fleece fabric
- String or ribbon

TIP! After a few weeks you may want to put in a fresh plastic bottle, to give it new crunch power!

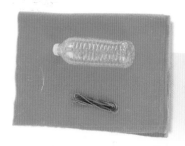

MAKE IT:

Dogs love crinkly, crunchy toys! Make this one from an empty water bottle.

1. Empty a plastic water bottle and then screw the cap on tight.
2. Cut a rectangle of fleece fabric that is about 12 by 28 inches (30 by 70 cm). Roll the bottle up in the fabric.
3. Use string to tie both sides, as close as you can to the water bottle.
4. Cut fringes on each end of the fabric. These will be fun for your dog to whip around!

GET YOUR DOG STARTED: When you give this toy to your dog, don't just hand it to him (that's no fun!). Crinkle it, skittle it around the floor, and play keep away with it. That will make him want to play with it!

2 Roll the bottle up in the fabric.

3 Tie both ends with string.

4 Cut fringes on the ends.

Dog Walking Depot

SUPPLIES
- Picture frame
- Dry-erase marker
- Velcro
- Leash hooks
- Small pail

MAKE IT:

Get organized with this handy dog walking station. It holds your dog's leash and treats, and has a message board to leave a note for mom.

1. Remove the glass from a picture frame and trace around it onto a piece of colored paper.

2. Cut out along the line you just drew. Write your dog's name on the paper or decorate it with photos or stickers. Leave space in the middle for erasable notes.

3. Insert your decorated paper and the glass back into the picture frame. Attach hooks to hang your dog's leash and a pail for biscuits.

FINISHING TOUCHES: Use Velcro to attach a dry-erase marker to the picture frame. With the marker you can write notes right on the glass.

1. Trace around the glass.

2. Cut it out.

3. Attach hooks and marker.

easy

Peekaboo

TROUBLESHOOTING

MY DOG IS SCARED TO GO BETWEEN MY LEGS

Never force your dog to do something she is afraid of or it will make her more afraid. Don't hold her collar. Keep offering her treats and she'll get a little braver each time.

TIP! Your dog wants you to be happy. Tell her what a good job she's doing!

TEACH IT:

In this slily trick your dog runs between your legs . . . peekaboo! (Let's just hope you don't have a Great Dane!)

1. Turn your back to your dog. Hold a treat between your legs and wiggle it to get your dog's attention. Say, "Peekaboo!"

2. As your dog sniffs or nibbles at the treat, bring it slowly forward so that your dog walks between your legs. If you move too quickly your dog will back out.

3. Once your dog is halfway through your legs, give her the treat.

4. Over time your dog will get braver, and will push through your legs. Don't forget to give her a treat every time.

WHAT TO EXPECT: Practice this trick every day and in a week your dog will be peekabooing. Don't be surprised if this becomes her favorite way of getting your attention!

1 Turn your back to your dog. Say, "Peekaboo!" and wiggle a treat between your legs.

2 Slowly bring the treat forward. If you move too quickly your dog will back out.

3 Let your dog nibble the treat from your hand.

4 Over time your dog will get braver and will push through faster.

Paws Up

BEFORE YOU START

Choose a stable stool, chair, or coffee table that won't tip over.

TROUBLESHOOTING

MY DOG WALKS AROUND THE STOOL, BUT WON'T STEP ON IT

Choose something lower for him to step on, like a drawer turned upside down.

MY DOG JUMPS OVER THE STOOL

This usually happens when you move your hand too quickly. Start at his nose and move your hand slowly over the stool.

HE STEPS ON IT WITH ONE PAW, BUT NOT TWO

He is cautious. Use a lower object for him to step on. At first, give him the treat for just one paw up, to get him interested in this trick.

TIP! Hold the treat between your fingers, with your hand flat, so your dog won't nip your fingers.

TEACH IT:

Teach your dog to put his front paws up onto a stool. This simple skill is the first step for all kinds of more complicated tricks, like walking on a balance beam (page 78).

1 Show your dog a treat near his nose. Slowly move it forward and up over the stool. Say, "Paws up!" and pat the stool to encourage him.

2 As he starts to reach for the treat, move it higher, just out of his reach. Move your hand slowly, or else he might try to jump over the stool.

3 He'll step onto the stool to reach for the treat. Hold the treat still and don't move it away from him anymore.

4 When he reaches the treat, tell him "good!" and let him take the treat from your hand.

WHAT TO EXPECT: This is an easy trick that most dogs can learn in a few days.

1 Move a treat from your dog's nose to over the stool. Pat the stool to encourage him up.

2 As your dog reaches for the treat, slowly move it higher, just out of his reach.

3 Hold your hand still and let your dog reach the treat.

4 Tell him "good!" and let him eat the treat.

easy

Guess Which Hand

BEFORE YOU START
Use a strong-smelling treat, like a piece of a hot dog or ham.

TROUBLESHOOTING

MY DOG SCRATCHES MY HAND
Dogs get excited when first learning this trick. You can wear gloves, or you can hold your hands higher so she can sniff them but can't reach them with her paws.

TIP! Microwave hot dog slices on a paper towel–covered plate for 3 minutes for a tasty training treat!

TEACH IT:

This is a fun game to play with your dog. Hide a treat in one hand and ask your dog to "guess which hand." If she gets it right, she gets the treat!

1. Hold a treat in one of your fists (but not too tightly, so your dog can still smell it). Hold out both fists to your dog and ask her, "Which hand?"

2. Your dog will probably sniff both of your hands, and then decide which one she thinks has the treat. She'll then sniff that hand more, and may even paw at it.

3. If she chose correctly, say, "Good!" and open your hand to let her have the treat.

4. If your dog chose incorrectly, open the hand she chose to show her that it is empty. Then try the game again.

WHAT TO EXPECT: Dogs usually enjoy this game and catch on pretty quickly. They are often excited though, and may have trouble staying calm.

1 Show your dog both of your fists and ask her, "Which hand?"

2 Wait for your dog to show interest in one of your hands, by sniffing or pawing at it.

3 Say, "Good!" and open your hand.

4 If your dog chose incorrectly, open your hand to show her that it is empty.

Duffle Jump

BEFORE YOU START

Make sure the ground has good traction and is not slippery. Grass is the best surface.

TROUBLESHOOTING

MY DOG TRIPPED ON THE JUMP AND NOW HE IS SCARED OF IT

Don't make a big deal out of it when it happens. Go back to a lower height for a while.

MY DOG RUNS AROUND THE JUMP, AND NOT OVER IT

If your dog is trying to sneak around the side of the jump instead of over it, place the side of the jump next to a wall so he can't go around it.

TIP! Arrange several jumps in a row. Can you take your dog through the whole line of jumps?

TEACH IT:

How high can you jump? Start small, and work your way up to the top.

1   Start with a low duffle jump (build a jump with instructions on page 66). With your dog on a lead, jog with him toward the jump and give an enthusiastic "hup!" as you jump over the bar with him. Praise him and give him a treat. If your dog is reluctant, lower the bar to the ground and walk over it with him (but don't pull him over it). Give him lots of encouragement.

2   As your dog gets more confident, raise the height of the jump. Run alongside your dog now, and not over the jump. Make sure he has plenty of loose leash so you are not pulling his collar.

3   Can your dog go higher? Raise your arm up and over the jump to get his energy up.

WHAT TO EXPECT: Most dogs enjoy jumping and will take to it easily when given excited praise. Within a few days your dog can be a jumper!

1 Put a lead on your dog and jog with him over the jump.

2 Try a higher jump. Run alongside it now, and not over it.

Build a duffle jump (page 66).

3 Use your arm to guide your dog where you want him to go.

William Potter, I don't think you're even trying!

easy

Build a Duffle Jump

SUPPLIES
- PVC pipe (1 inch, 25 mm)
- 2 PVC elbows (1 inch, 25 mm)
- 2 PVC T-joints (1 inch, 25 mm)
- PVC cutting tool or saw

You can find these items in the outdoor irrigation section of your hardware or gardening store.

TROUBLESHOOTING

HOW HIGH SHOULD I MAKE MY JUMP?
Athletic dogs will be able to jump the same height as their shoulder. When first teaching your dog to jump, start at a height about half the height of his elbow.

TIP! If you find that your dog is knocking the jump over or hitting it with his back legs, make a shorter jump.

BUILD IT:

Build your own duffle jump, and teach your dog to **jump over it** (page 64)!

1. Cut your pipe with a PVC cutting tool or a saw. The length of the uprights will determine how tall your jump will be. This will vary depending on the size of your dog.
2. Assemble the two feet by pressing the pipes into the T-joints. Pound it on the ground a few times to get a tight fit.
3. Assemble the two uprights.
4. Insert each upright into a foot. Lastly, insert the crossbar into the uprights.
5. In dog sport competition, jumps are decorated with colored tape to make them easier for the dogs to see.

FINISHING TOUCHES: Add some color to your jumps with a type of paint made for outdoor plastic patio furniture!

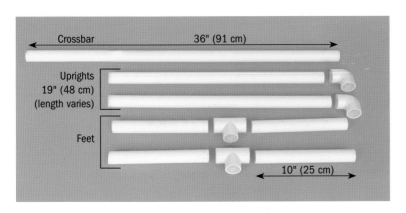

Crossbar — 36" (91 cm)

Uprights
19" (48 cm)
(length varies)

Feet

10" (25 cm)

1 Use a PVC cutting tool to cut your pipe. The length of the uprights is determined by the size of your dog.

2 Assemble the feet.

3 Assemble the uprights

4 Insert each upright into a foot, and then attach the crossbar.

Teach your dog to jump over your jump (page 64).

5 Decorate your jump with colored tape to make it easier for your dog to see.

Ring the Doorbell to Go Out

BEFORE YOU START

Make a set of doggy doorbells (page 70)

TROUBLESHOOTING

WHEN MY DOG WANTS TO GO OUT SHE STARES AT THE DOOR AND DOESN'T RING THE BELL

Walk over, put a dab of peanut butter on the bell, wait for her to ring it, and then let her out. She'll soon make the connection.

TIP! Hang doggy doorbells on the outside of doors too, so your dog can let you know when she wants to come back in.

TEACH IT:

Does your dog have to go out? Teach her to ring a bell to let you know . . . how convenient!

1 Hang a bell from your doorknob at a low height. Dab a bit of peanut butter on the bell.

2 Point it out to your dog and say "jingle!" When she goes to sniff it or lick it, it will jingle softly.

3 As soon as you hear the jingle, say "good!" and give her a treat.

4 After a few repetitions, your dog will probably have licked all the peanut butter off, but don't add more. Simply touch the bell or point to it and say "jingle." Give her a treat if she makes it jingle. If she seems confused, go back to using the peanut butter a few more times.

5 Get your dog excited to go for a walk. Stop at the door and encourage her to ring the bell. It may take a while, but as soon as she touches the bell open the door and let her outside. Use the peanut butter again if you have to.

WHAT TO EXPECT: In the beginning, be very responsive to your dog's jingling and open the door every time she rings the bell. Dogs, even puppies, catch on quickly and learn to jingle the bell when they need to go out.

1 Dab a bit of peanut butter on the bell.

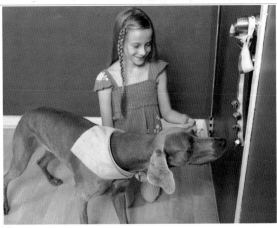

2 When your dog sniffs it, it will jingle.

3 Say "good!" and give her a treat.

4 Don't add more peanut butter. Simply point to the bell and encourage her to jingle it.

5 Get your dog excited to go for a walk. Have her jingle the bell before opening the door.

Make a set of doggy doorbells (page 70).

Make a Doggy Doorbell

SUPPLIES
- Shoelace
- A belt
- Several jingle bells
- Ribbon

TIP! Does your dog have an old collar that he no longer wears? If it has holes, you can repurpose it as a doggy doorbell!

MAKE IT:

Recycle an old belt into a doggy doorbell! Teach your dog to ring it when he has to go out, with the instructions on page 68

1. Tie a knot at one end of a shoelace. Poke the other end through the first hole in your belt (poking from the back side of the belt to the front side).

2. Lace it through a jingle bell and back down through the next hole in the belt. Keep repeating, in and out, until you have all of your bells strung.

3. At the end, tie a knot in the shoelace to secure it.

4. Cut the belt approximately in half to shorten it. Round the corners to make it pretty.

5. Punch a hole at the top of the belt using a punch tool or a nail.

6. String a ribbon through the top hole, and tie it around the door handle.

FINISHING TOUCHES: Adjust the height of the bells by shortening or lengthening the ribbon. Your dog should be able touch them with his nose while standing.

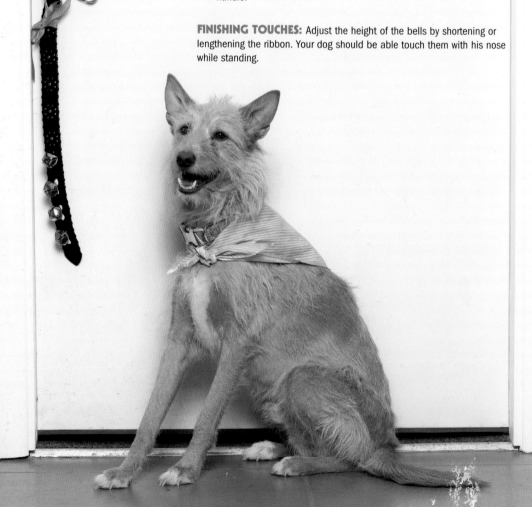

1 String your shoelace through the first belt hole.

2 Lace it through a jingle bell, and back down through the next belt hole. Repeat for each bell.

3 At the end, secure it with a knot.

4 Cut the belt to shorten it.

5 Punch a hole near the top.

Teach your dog to ring the bells when he has to go out (page 68).

6 String a ribbon through the hole and tie it to the doorknob.

Tunnel

BEFORE YOU START

Use a kids play tunnel for small dogs, or an agility tunnel for larger dogs.

TROUBLESHOOTING

MY DOG IS AFRAID OF THE TUNNEL

Put several really yummy treats inside the tunnel and let him explore it on his own.

MY DOG GOES AROUND THE TUNNEL, NOT THROUGH IT

The kid at the tunnel entrance has an important job. Don't push the dog in the tunnel, but hold him until he is making eye contact with the treat, and then let him go.

TIP! Leave the tunnel set up for a few days so that your dog can explore it on his own and get over any fear of it.

TEACH IT:

Going through a tunnel can be scary at first, but with your patience and encouragement your dog will come out the other side a more confident dog.

1. Collapse the tunnel so it is very short and put a sand bag inside to keep it steady. Have one kid at the tunnel entrance holding the dog, and another kid at the tunnel exit (don't sit too close to the exit or your dog won't feel like he has room to come out). The kid at the exit makes eye contact with the dog through the tunnel, calls him, and holds out a treat toward him.

2. It may take several minutes of coaxing . . . be patient. When your dog finally goes through the tunnel, give him the treat.

3. Expand the tunnel so it is longer. Try the same thing again. If your dog is scared, go back to the shorter tunnel.

4. Give your dog the treat as soon as he exits. Leave enough room at the exit so that he does not feel trapped in the tunnel.

WHAT TO EXPECT: Some dogs will go through the tunnel pretty easily, and some are more afraid of the tunnel. If your dog is afraid, don't force him through (or his fear will double!). Give him the time he needs to explore the tunnel on his own. Once accustomed to it, most dogs really enjoy running through the tunnel.

1   Make eye contact with your dog and hold out a treat. Leave room for him to exit.

2   When he goes through the tunnel, give him the treat.

3   Expand the tunnel and try the same thing again.

4   Give him a treat as he exits. Leave room so he can exit easily.

Touch My Hand

TROUBLESHOOTING

I'M AFRAID MY DOG WILL BITE MY HAND

There are only two things you can do that might make your dog nip you hand. One is not holding your hand flat (if it's flat, he can't bite it). The other is pulling your hand away quickly at the last second—this can make your dog want to chase your hand, like he would chase a fly. Don't do either of those things.

TIP! Don't move your hand toward your dog's nose. Hold your hand still and wait for his nose to come to your hand.

TEACH IT:

Did your puppy run off? Hold out your hand and call "touch!" to see him race back to you!

1. Wedge a treat between your fingers. Hold your hand flat, with your palm toward your dog. Hold your hand at your dog's nose height.

2. Say "touch!" and wiggle your hand to try to get your dog interested in the treat.

3. The second you feel his nose touch your hand, say "good!" and let him take the treat. Repeat this step a few times.

4. Once your dog gets the hang of this, try it with no treat between your fingers. Hold out your hand and say "touch!" The instant your dog touches your hand, say "good!" and give him a treat from your pocket.

WHAT TO EXPECT: Dogs love this game and catch on quickly. Practice ten times per day and within a few days your dog will be doing this trick!

1. Wedge a treat between your fingers. Hold your hand flat, at your dog's nose height.

2. Wiggle your hand a bit and encourage your dog to investigate the treat.

3. The second you feel his nose touch your hand, say "good!" and let him take the treat.

4. Try it with no treat between your fingers. When your dog touches your hand, say "good!" and give him a treat from your pocket.

Touch a Target Stick

BEFORE YOU START

It will be helpful to first teach your dog to **touch your hand** (page 74).

TROUBLESHOOTING

MY DOG BITES THE STICK

Dogs will first lick the stick before they bite it. The second he licks it, say "good!" and give him a treat. That way he won't have time to bite it.

TIP! Make a target stick from a wooden spoon. Dip the end in paint to make it a visible target for your dog.

TEACH IT:

Teach your dog to touch a stick with his nose. Move the stick around and watch your dog follow it.

1. Put some treats in your pocket. Dab a bit of peanut butter on the end of your target stick.

2. Hold out the stick to your dog. He will want to lick the peanut butter.

3. The second he touches it (with his nose or tongue), say "good!" and give him a treat from your pocket.

4. After a few repetitions, try it without the peanut butter. The target stick will probably still smell a little like peanut butter, which should be enough to get your dog to sniff it. The instant he touches it, say "good!" and give him a treat.

WHAT TO EXPECT: Dogs learn this trick pretty quickly. Once your dog has the hang of this game, place the target stick at different heights, both high and low. Have your dog follow a moving target by guiding the target stick away from him, or around in a circle.

1. Put a dab of peanut butter on your target stick.

2. Hold it out for your dog. He'll want to lick the peanut butter.

3. As soon as he touches the target stick, say "good!" and pull out a treat from your pocket.

4. Now try it without the peanut butter. Will your dog still touch it?

Balance Beam

BEFORE YOU START

It will be helpful to first teach your dog to put his paws up (page 60).

TROUBLESHOOTING

MY DOG WON'T PUT HER FRONT PAWS UP

Practice the **paws up** trick (page 60) and have her put her paws up on all sorts of objects.

MY DOG WON'T BRING HER BACK PAWS UP

Don't touch your dog's back paws or lift her onto the bench. Put the bench alongside a wall. Move the treat over the bench, and use your body to block her from turning perpendicular to the bench.

MY DOG JUMPS OFF IN THE MIDDLE

Have a whole handful of treats and give her a treat every second. If she jumps off, she stops getting treats.

TIP! Put the bench close to a wall, so she can't jump off or turn sideways.

TEACH IT:

Can your dog walk across a balance beam like a gymnast? With a little help from you, I'll bet she can!

1   Start with a picnic bench, as it is stable and pretty wide. (Little dogs may need a stepping stool to help them get onto the bench.) Hold a treat to your dog's nose and move it slowly above the bench to get her to put her front paws up. Give her a treat the second her front paws are up.

2   Continue to slowly move your treat forward, drawing your dog along. It's important to keep your dog pointed forward. If she turns sideways to the bench, she won't put her back feet on it.

3   Once she is up, slowly move your hand forward. Keep your hand low so your dog can still see the beam while watching your treat. Give her a treat every few steps.

4   Give her a treat at the end, before she jumps off. Do not give treats after she has jumped off (or your dog will think she got a treat for being *off* the beam).

5   Once your dog has the hang of the picnic bench, try a slightly skinnier beam like a board (build a simple balance beam with the instructions on page 80).

WHAT TO EXPECT: The initial teaching of this trick is the hardest. Once you get your dog to do it the first time, then you've got it made. What often happens is that the dog puts only her front paws on the beam and walks along the beam that way (silly dog!). Read the troubleshooting box for helpful suggestions.

1 Move a treat from your dog's nose to above the bench.

2 Continue to slowly move your treat forward. Keep your dog pointed forward.

3 Walk alongside your dog, giving her treats every few steps.

4 Give her a treat at the end, BEFORE she jumps off.

5 Try a skinnier balance beam, such as a board.

Build your own balance beam (page 80).

Build a Balance Beam

SUPPLIES

- 8 cement blocks
  6 x 8 x 16 inches (140 x 215 x 440 mm)
  The hole in the block is
  6½ inches wide (165 mm)

- A standard-size board
  6 x 2 inches x 10 feet (150 x 50 mm x 3 m)

These standard building materials can be found at your home improvement store.

TIP! Wear gloves when building this balance beam, as the bricks are quite heavy.

BUILD IT:

Build this sturdy, safe balance beam for your dog. And the best part is, there's no hammer, no nails, and no power tools!

1. Set out two pairs of blocks, parallel to each other, with about 6 feet (2 m) of space between the pairs. Arrange them nice and snug together, on a sturdy ground surface. Watch out, they are heavier than they look!

2. Put the other four blocks on top, but facing the other direction. Did I mention they are heavy?

3. Lay your board on top of the blocks. Slide one end through the holes and push it so that it comes out the other end.

4. Slide the other end of the board through the holes in the other stack of blocks. Adjust it so the board is even within both sets of blocks. Pretty cool!

FINISHING TOUCHES: If your small dog needs help climbing onto the blocks, add another block at each end to act as a step.

1 Arrange two pairs of blocks with 6 feet (2 m) of space between them.

2 Add another set of blocks on top, facing the other direction.

3 Lay your board on top of your block stacks. Slide one end through the holes in the blocks.

4 Slide the other end of the board through the holes in the other side.

Teach your dog to walk a balance beam (page 78).

Spin Circles

TROUBLESHOOTING

MY DOG DOESN'T FOLLOW MY HAND
Are you using a really good treat? Try "people food" like hot dogs, chicken, ham, or cheese.

MY DOG GOES ONLY HALFWAY
Reaching your hand too far forward too fast will cause the circle to stall. Start close to your stomach and move your hand to the side before reaching it forward.

TIP! Teach this trick in both directions. For the other side, say "around," hold the treat in your left hand, and move it to your left side.

TEACH IT:

Teach your dog to spin circles. Whoa, you're making me dizzy!

1. Hold a treat in your right hand. Face your dog and get him interested in your treat.

2. Say "spin," and move your right hand to your right. Your dog's nose will follow your hand.

3. Continue moving your hand forward so you make a large circle. Keep your hand low, at your dog's nose height, and move slowly so that you don't lose your dog.

4. Once your dog has followed your hand all the way around your circle, open your hand and let him have the treat.

WHAT TO EXPECT: As your dog improves, start to make smaller and faster circles with your treat. Eventually you won't need a treat at all in your hand (although you should still give your dog a treat from your pocket at the end). Practice ten times per day and in a week your dog will be spinning circles!

1 Hold a treat in your right hand and let your dog sniff it.

2 Move your right hand to your right, keeping it at your dog's nose height.

3 Continue to move your treat in a large circle.

4 At the end of the circle, open your hand and let your dog have the treat. Good job!

Hoop Jump

BEFORE YOU START

Remove the noisy beads from your hoop to make it less frightening for your dog.

TROUBLESHOOTING

THE HOOP FELL ON MY DOG AND NOW SHE IS FRIGHTENED OF IT!

Dogs pick up on your energy, so don't make a big fuss over it. Put the hoop back down to ground level and have her walk through it a few times.

TIP! Decorate your hoop with art tape to make it into a circus hoop.

TEACH IT:

Teach your dog to jump through a hoop like a circus dog!

1. Your dog may be frightened of the hoop at first, so give her time to investigate it. Hold the hoop on the ground using the hand closest to your dog. Hold several treats in your other hand. Slowly lure her through the hoop by giving her treats with every step she takes.

2. Raise the hoop a little and try again. If your dog gets tangled in the hoop, just drop the hoop.

3. If your dog keeps trying to go around the hoop instead of through it, hold the hoop across a doorway.

4. Raise the hoop again so that your dog must jump to get through it. Tell her "hup!" to get her excited to jump.

WHAT TO EXPECT: Dogs usually get the hang of hoop jumping within a few days and do it enthusiastically. Don't forget to give her a treat to keep her motivated.

1 Hold the hoop on the ground using the hand closest to your dog. With your other hand, use a treat to lure your dog through.

2 Raise the hoop a little and try again. Be prepared to drop the hoop if your dog gets tangled.

3 If your dog is trying to go around the hoop, put it in a doorway.

4 Say an enthusiastic "hup!" to get her energized to jump! Give her a treat every time she jumps through.

Kennel Up

BEFORE YOU START
Make your dog's kennel comfortable with clean, soft bedding and a toy inside.

TROUBLESHOOTING
I DON'T HAVE A CRATE. MY DOG SLEEPS IN A DOG BED.
You can teach this trick the exact same way with a dog bed.

TIP! Your dog's kennel is his personal place that he goes to when he wants to be left alone. Don't crawl into his kennel or reach inside.

TEACH IT:

Your dog needs a special crate or dog bed that is his very own. Teach him a name for his kennel so you can send him there for bedtime.

1. Toss a treat in your dog's crate as you tell him to "kennel up." When he goes in after the treat, say "good kennel up." Do this a couple of times a day for several days.

2. By now he will be pretty excited to kennel up when you tell him to. This time, say "kennel up" and *pretend* to toss a treat into his kennel.

3. Once he goes in the crate, say "good kennel up" and hand him a treat. Be sure to give the treat while he is still inside the crate. (If you were to give him the treat after he came out of the kennel, he would think he earned a treat for coming *out* of his kennel—not what we want!)

4. As he gets better, you can stand farther away when you send him to his kennel. Then walk over and give him a treat in his crate.

WHAT TO EXPECT: As part of his bedtime routine your dog will look forward to kenneling up and receiving his goodnight treat.

1. Toss a treat in his kennel and say "kennel up."

2. Say "kennel up" and pretend to toss a treat into his kennel.

3. Give him a treat while he is still in his crate.

4. As he gets better, stand farther away when you say "kennel up."

Test: Right-Pawed or Left-Pawed

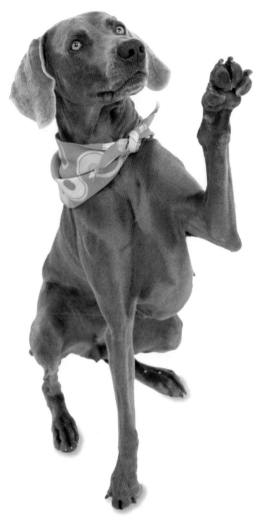

TEACH IT:

Dogs can be right-pawed or left-pawed (just like people can be right-handed or left-handed). Which paw does your dog favor? Test her to find out.

1 Give your dog a treat-dispensing toy to play with. Which paw does she use most often?

2 Stick a piece of tape to the center of your dog's head or muzzle. Which paw does she use to get it off?

3 Give your dog a bone or peanut butter–filled toy. Which paw does she use to hold it?

4 Put a treat or toy under the sofa. Which paw does your dog use to reach for it?

TIP! Although most people are right-handed, dogs are equally right- and left-handed.

WHAT TO EXPECT: As with humans, your dog will use both paws, but she will use one a little more than the other. Watch your dog over a period of time and see if you can figure out which is her dominant side. Here are some more ways you can test your dog's paw preference: When she gets on or off of something, which paw does she step with first? When she wants your attention, which paw does she use to paw your leg? When she chases a lizard, which paw does she try to step on it with?

Bark the Answer

TEACH IT:

"Buddy, how old are you?" Ruff! Ruff! Ruff! "That's right, you're three!"
Teach your dog to bark on cue.

1. Most dogs bark at the sound of the doorbell, so we'll use that. Stand at your front door with the door open (so your dog will be able to hear the doorbell). Say "bark!" in a voice that kind of sounds like a bark and press the doorbell.

2. If your dog barks, say "good bark!" and give him a treat. Repeat this about six times.

3. On the seventh time, say "bark!" and pretend to ring the doorbell, but don't actually ring it. You may have to say "bark!" a few more times. If your dog does bark, act all excited and give him a treat. If he doesn't bark, go back to ringing the doorbell.

WHAT TO EXPECT: If your dog likes to bark at doorbells, then he can learn this trick in one session. Once you are able to just say "bark" and have him bark, the next step is to move a little away from the front door (your dog will be a little confused at first). Don't forget to give a treat every time.

TROUBLESHOOTING

MY DOG DOESN'T BARK AT THE DOORBELL

Is there something else that makes him bark? Try having a friend knock on your door or tap a window with a metal key. (Works best if your dog doesn't see your friend.)

1. Say "bark!" in a barky kind of voice, and ring the doorbell.

2. When your dog barks, immediately say "good bark!" and give him a treat.

3. Say "bark!" and just pretend to ring the doorbell. Did he bark?

Open the Door

BEFORE YOU START
Small dogs can open a cabinet door instead of a full-size door.

TROUBLESHOOTING

MY DOG ISN'T INTERESTED IN THE DISH TOWEL
Use smellier treats inside, such as steak, chicken, ham, and liver.

TIP! Some dogs have been known to swallow towels (crazy, but true!). Don't leave the dish towel unattended if it smells like treats.

TEACH IT:

Ding dong . . . "Just a second, my dog will answer the door." Teach your dog to pull on a dish towel to open the door. That's useful!

1. Take the corner of a dish towel and tie some treats up in a knot. Wiggle it around your dog to get him interested in it.

2. Tie the dish towel to the doorknob. Show your dog the end with the treats.

3. Your dog will sniff and lick the towel. Encourage him by saying, "Get it! Open the door!" Eventually he will pull on it a bit, and the door will move.

4. Immediately say "good!" and give him a treat from your pocket.

WHAT TO EXPECT: Dogs learn this trick pretty quickly! Eventually, when your dog is doing it well, take the treats out of the dish towel and just give him a treat from your pocket when he pulls the door open.

1. Tie some treats in a knotted dish towel, and wiggle it in front of your dog.

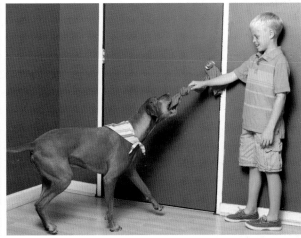

2. Tie it to the doorknob and show your dog the end with the treats.

3. Encourage your dog to "open the door!" When he pulls the dish towel, the door will move.

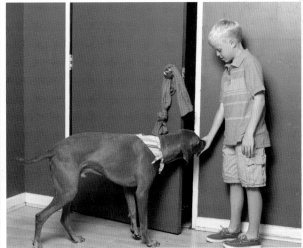

4. Immediately say "good!" and give him a treat from your pocket.

Box Search

BEFORE YOU START
Gather several large cardboard boxes—they can be different sizes.

TROUBLESHOOTING

MY DOG LOSES INTEREST AND WALKS AWAY

Dogs are sensitive. She's not sure what she's supposed to do, so she is giving up. Make it easier for your dog for a while until she is confident with what you want from her.

TIP! If your dog is having trouble smelling the treat, put a bowl with a whole handful of treats inside the box. When she finds it, give her just one of the treats.

TEACH IT:

Police dogs and security dogs are trained to do box searches to look for hidden items. Dogs at the airport search suitcases. Your dog can learn this trick, too!

1. Set out a few open boxes. Put a treat in one, and mix them up so your dog doesn't know which box has the "hide."

2. Tell your dog to "find it!" Let her eat the treat when she finds it.

3. This time partially close the boxes. Your dog will have to search a little harder to find the "hide."

4. Close the lids all the way this time, so your dog won't be able to get the treat herself. Poke holes in the boxes so she will still be able to smell their contents.

5. Watch your dog carefully. When it looks like she is paying attention to the correct box, say "good!" Open the lid for her and give her one of the treats inside.

WHAT TO EXPECT: The reason we close the lids and no longer allow the dog to take the treats herself is that we are training her to work like a police dog. Police dogs must show their handler where the item is, but not eat it.

1. Hide a treat in one of the boxes.

2. Tell your dog to "find it!"

3. Partially close the boxes and try again.

4. Close the lids all the way. Poke holes in the boxes so your dog can smell them.

5. When your dog is paying extra attention to the correct box, open the lid and give her a treat.

easy

Commando Crawl

BEFORE YOU START
You can use chairs or a coffee table for this trick.

TROUBLESHOOTING

MY DOG BACKS OUT OF THE CHAIRS
Your dog may initially try to back out of the chairs. That's okay, let him do it. Just try again, and he'll be a little more confident each time.

TIP! Your dog will be much more willing to crawl on a comfortable surface such as grass or carpet.

TEACH IT:

Teach your dog to crawl on his belly under a row of chairs, just like an army commando might.

1. Start with one chair. Put the side of a chair against the wall, so your dog can't crawl out that side. Sit on the other side of the chair so your dog can't crawl out that side either. Use a treat to coax his head under the chair.

2. Tell your dog "crawl" and keep pulling the treat slowly forward. Don't move too fast, or your dog will back out.

3. As your dog comes out the other side, give him the treat.

4. Now try it with two chairs. Hold treats in both of your hands, so you don't have to switch hands halfway through. Give your dog treats along the way.

5. Three chairs? Give it a try! Give your dog treats along the way and one at the end.

WHAT TO EXPECT: Crawling is hard work for a dog, so do only a few repetitions at a time.

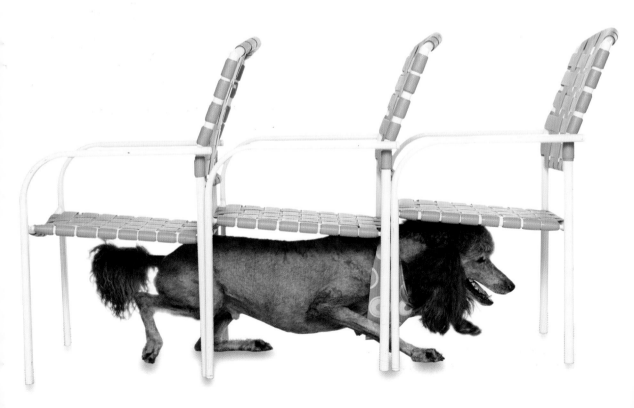

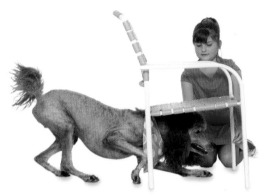

1 Put a chair against a wall, and sit on the opposite side to prevent your dog from going out the sides.

2 Tell your dog to "crawl" and pull the treat forward.

3 Give your dog the treat as when he comes out.

4 Use two chairs. Hold treats in both hands and give him pieces along the way.

5 Can your dog do three chairs? Keep giving him treats along the way, and a big one at the end.

Be a Tree

BEFORE YOU START
Practice this technique on your own or with your parent before you try it with a dog.

TROUBLESHOOTING

HOW LONG DO I HAVE TO STAY BEING A TREE?

Until the dog has lost interest and walks away. If you move and the dog gets interested in you again, go back to being a tree.

MORE SAFETY TIPS

- Don't stare a dog in the eyes
- Don't put your face up to a dog's face
- Don't try to take something away from a dog
- Don't go near a dog who is eating or chewing something
- Don't approach a dog that is on a bed or furniture
- Don't approach a dog that is tied up or in a car
- Don't pet a dog through a fence or in a kennel
- Don't climb over a fence into a dog's yard (even if the dog is usually friendly)
- Never try to break up a dog fight or interact with dogs that are play fighting
- Leave dogs alone if they are sleeping, injured, very old, or with puppies

LEARN IT:

Use this technique when you want a dog to leave you alone, such as when he is jumping on you or chasing you, or if you encounter a scary dog on the street. A dog has no interest in a tree, so act like a tree and the dog will leave you alone.

1. **Stop.** Dogs like to chase things and the more you run, the more the dog will want to chase you. Stop and plant your roots.

2. **Fold in your branches.** Kids' hands smell yummy. If you raise your hands the dog will jump on you trying to sniff your hands. Instead, keep your hands down and folded so the dog can sniff them easily. Don't make a fist, because the dog may think you are holding a treat and try to open your fist.

3. **Watch your roots grow.** By being still and avoiding eye contact you are showing the dog that you are not going to threaten him or play with him.

4. If the dog knocks you over, cover your head and "be a rock."

WHAT TO EXPECT: The "be a tree" technique is extremely effective and is the best way to react to any dog who makes you uncomfortable.

1 Stop.

2 Fold in your branches.

3 Watch your roots grow.

4 If the dog knocks you over, cover your head and "be a rock."

I can be a tree too!

Hide Your Head Under a Cushion

BEFORE YOU START
Use a chair that has a seat cushion tied to its back.

TROUBLESHOOTING

MY DOG DOESN'T PUT HER HEAD UNDER THE CUSHION
She probably doesn't know there's a treat under there. Hold up the cushion and point to the treat.

TIP! For little dogs use a large cushion on the floor.

TEACH IT:

Are you playing hide-and-seek? Have your dog hide her head under a cushion.

1. Show your dog as you put a treat under the cushion, near the front.

2. Hold the cushion slightly up. Tell your dog to "hide your head!" and let her poke her head underneath to get the treat. Gradually place the treat farther toward the rear of the cushion, so that your dog has to bury her entire head underneath to get it.

3. Stand behind the chair and hold the treat in your hand, under the cushion.

4. Tell your dog to "hide your head!" Give her the treat from your hand while her head is under the cushion.

5. Eventually your dog will be able to hide her head without any treat under the cushion. When she does, give her a treat from your pocket.

WHAT TO EXPECT: This trick is pretty easy to teach, but you have to use baby steps. It's not the easiest thing in the world for your dog to figure out how to put her head under a cushion.

1 Put a treat under the chair cushion.

2 Hold the cushion up slightly so your dog can poke her head under to get the treat.

3 Stand behind the chair and hold a treat under the cushion.

4 Give your dog the treat from your hand.

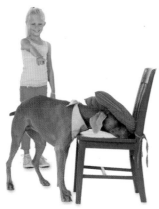

5 Eventually just point to the chair and tell your dog to "hide your head!"

Stamp Pad Paw Art

SUPPLIES
- Stamp pad (washable ink)
- Art paper
- Clipboard
- Marker

TROUBLESHOOTING

HOW DO I GET THE INK OFF HIS PAWS?
Washable ink comes off easily. Let your dog run around outside for a few minutes and the ink will come off by itself.

TIP! Use a rainbow stamp pad to make extra colorful paw prints.

MAKE IT:

Every dog's paw print is unique. Use a stamp pad to turn your dog's paw print into art.

1. Do this art project outdoors, just in case your dog runs off with inky paws (moms don't always understand the artistic process). Get your stamp pad ready. Gently take one of your dog's paws, holding it by the wrist. Don't lift it very far off the ground. Bring the stamp pad up to your dog's paw (instead of trying to push your dog's paw down into the pad).

2. Put your art paper on a clipboard so it has a hard surface. Bring the paper up to the paw to make a paw stamp.

FINISHING TOUCHES: Use a marker to write your dog's name below his artwork.

1. Hold your dog's wrist near the ground. Bring the stamp pad up to his paw.

2. Bring the clipboard up to meet the paw.

Add your dog's name to his art.

Rainbow Toes

MAKE IT:

Tired of boring old paw prints? Make something really original with this rainbow print.

1. Get your supplies ready and close by: several colors of paint poured onto a plate and your art paper. Have someone help you by holding your dog's collar. Lift your dog's paw by holding just below his ankle. Bend his paw back so you can see it.

2. Dip your finger in the paint and touch it onto one of your dog's toes. Get all around the edges. Dip your finger in another color of paint and do another toe, and another toe. Be careful to not let your dog's paw drop during all of this painting.

3. Now the tricky part: Carefully guide your dog's paw down to the paper. Your helper should gently push on your dog's side, so he is off balance and forced to put his weight on that paw. If you don't do this, your dog won't put any weight on the "icky" paw.

FINISHING TOUCHES: Did it work? Wow, I'm impressed! This is a tough painting and it may take a couple of tries to get it right.

SUPPLIES
- Several colors of washable paint
- Art paper

1. Hold just below the ankle and bend the paw back.

2. Use your finger to paint on one of your dog's toes.

3. Guide your dog's paw down as your helper leans your dog toward you.

Paw Posies

SUPPLIES
- Washable paint
- Paintbrush
- Disposable plate or bowl
- Art paper
- Clipboard or cookie sheet
- Masking tape
- Bowl of warm water
- Marker

TROUBLESHOOTING

THE PAWPRINTS AREN'T PERFECT
   Not every paw print will turn out perfectly, but that's what makes it special and unique.

TIP! We use washable paint for this project, but just to be on the safe side you'd probably better do this outside.

MAKE IT:

In this joint art piece your dog makes the flowers and you add the leaves and stems.

1. Before you start, get your materials ready. Pick a bright color of paint and pour it into a disposable plate or bowl. Tape your art paper to something sturdy like a clipboard or a cookie sheet. Set out a bowl filled with warm water to wash off those little paws after your dog is done painting.

2. Lift your dog's paw by holding it just above his ankle. Lift the plate of paint up to his paw (don't try to push his paw down into the plate as your dog will resist).

3. Lift the paper up to his paw and press for several seconds. Bring the paper straight down to avoid smudging. Whew, the hard part is done! While the paint is drying, rinse off your dog's paw in the warm water.

4. Pretend the paw prints are the petals of flowers and add the stems and leaves. Put a yellow dot in the center where the pollen would be.

FINISHING TOUCHES: Write your dog's name on his painting. Good job making this painting together!

2 Hold your dog's paw above his ankle and lift the paint up to his paw.

3 Bring the paper up to the paw and straight down again.

4 Pretend the paw prints are flower petals. Add the stems, leaves, and pollen spot.

Sign your names to your art.

No-Mess Paw Painting

SUPPLIES
- Three colors of paint
- Canvas
- Paper towels
- Plastic wrap

TROUBLESHOOTING

I CAN'T GET MY DOG TO WALK ON THE CANVAS

Having trouble getting your dog to walk across the canvas? Teach your dog **paws up** (page 60).

TIP! There is no wrong way to make art. Here are some ideas: use colors that match the color scheme of your room. Or drizzle a different color in each corner of your canvas. Add some hand prints along with the paw prints.

MAKE IT:

Make a masterpiece with your dog—don't worry, mom, this one is no mess, guaranteed!

1 Choose three colors of paint: one dark color and two brighter colors. Drizzle the darkest color onto your canvas first, then drizzle each of the other colors.

2 You'll want to have a good amount of paint drizzled. Be sure to get all the corners drizzled as well.

3 Lay three layers of paper towels on top of your canvas.

4 Wrap the whole thing in plastic wrap. Wrap it just about as tight as you would wrap a ham sandwich.

5 Hold a treat in front of your dog's nose and slowly move it away from him and toward the canvas, to get him to walk across the canvas. Have him walk across the canvas several times.

6 Unwrap the plastic wrap, remove the paper towels, and voilà! Art!

FINISHING TOUCHES: Lay your painting flat to dry for a full day. Don't leaving it standing up or the paint will slide down the canvas.

1. Drizzle paint onto your canvas, starting with the darkest color.

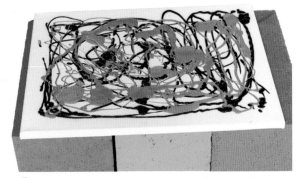

2. Do one color at a time. Be sure to get all corners of your canvas.

3. Lay three layers of paper towels on top of the paint.

4. Wrap the whole thing up like a ham sandwich.

5. Use a treat to get your dog to step on the painting.

6. Unwrap your masterpiece!

Collar Studs

SUPPLIES
- Large brads (brads come in two sizes)
- Nail polish
- Toothpick

TROUBLESHOOTING

IT'S TOO HARD TO DRAW WITH THE TOOTHPICK
You can use a paint pen or permanent marker instead. They come in a variety of colors, too.

TIP! Here's a fun idea: paint one letter of your dog's name onto each stud.

MAKE IT:

Show off your dog's personality with these unique collar studs! Change them out to suit the day.

1. Poke your brads into something to hold them upright. You can use an egg carton, a raw potato, or an apple.

2. Paint the entire top of the brads with nail polish. Let them dry for ten minutes.

3. Dip a toothpick into the nail polish bottle and carefully draw on your stud. Make polka dots, a heart, a happy face, or whatever you want.

4. Put the brad through one of the open holes on your dog's collar. Bend the ends outward and then back to the middle so the pointy part won't hurt your dog. You may have to fold the ends a second time if they are still too long.

FINISHING TOUCHES: Make a heart design. Use a toothpick to put two drops of nail polish next to each other. Touch one of the drops and slide your toothpick down at an angle. Repeat with the other drop. You did it!

1 Poke your brads into an egg carton to hold them up.

2 Paint the brads with colored nail polish.

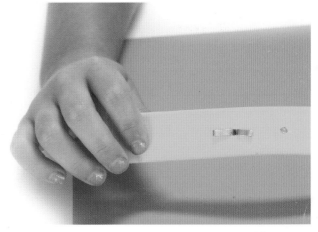

3 Use a toothpick to draw a design on the collar stud.

4 Poke it through an empty hole on your dog's collar. Bend the ends back to the middle.

To make a heart, start with two drops of nail polish. Touch one drop and slide your toothpick down at an angle. Repeat with the other drop.

Balance on a Brick

BEFORE YOU START

First teach your dog to put her **paws up** (page 60).

TROUBLESHOOTING

MY DOG WON'T PUT HER BACK FEET ON THE BRICKS

Move the treat forward so she puts her front feet on the bricks, and then keep moving it forward more. What will probably happen is that her front feet will come off the bricks at the same time that her back feet come on. Go ahead and give her a treat for that in the beginning. This teaches her that the trick has something to do with her back feet.

TIP! Paint your bricks in fun colors.

TEACH IT:

Teach your dog to fit all four paws on a teeny brick. Careful . . . don't lose your balance!

1. First teach your dog to put her **paws up** (page 60). Arrange four bricks into a large platform for your dog to stand on. Show her a treat and slowly move it up over the platform. As your dog reaches for it, keep moving the treat forward until she has all four paws on the platform. Say "good!" and let her take the treat.

2. Once she has the hang of this, take away one brick. Tell her to "step up" and use your treat to lure her forward. Only give her the treat when she has all four paws on the platform. If your dog keeps circling the platform, give her an occasional treat for just putting her front paws up so that she doesn't become discouraged and walk away. When she is doing it well, it's time to remove another brick.

3. Arrange two and a half bricks in a line, like a balance beam. This platform is narrower (which is harder than the last step), but also longer (which is easier). Stand to the side of the bricks and move your treat in a straight line.

4. Once she is doing it well, take away one brick. And when she has the hang of that, take away the half brick. Can she do it?

5. And finally, use just the teeny-tiny half brick. If she can do this, she's a superstar!

WHAT TO EXPECT: It takes a while for dogs to get the idea that their back feet have to be on the bricks. Resist the temptation to lift your dog's feet as this will make her not want to do the trick at all.

STEPS:

1 Move a treat forward until your dog has all four paws on the platform.

2 Take away a brick and tell her to "step up." Take away another brick.

3 Now arrange two and a half bricks in a narrow balance beam configuration.

4 Take away one brick. Then take a way the half brick.

William Potter, this is your best trick yet!

5 Use only the half brick. Now that's a trick!

Jump Over My Knee

BEFORE YOU START
Long pants are a good idea so you don't get accidentally scratched by your dog.

TROUBLESHOOTING

MY DOG WON'T EVEN WALK OVER MY LEGS
Cautious dogs may not want to even step on your thigh. Lure him slowly with a treat until he places his front paws on your thigh. Allow him to nibble the treat from this position.

TIP! In an enthusiastic voice, say "hup!" to get a higher jump!

TEACH IT:

Kneel on the floor and have your dog jump over your knee. Don't forget to smile!

1. Sit on the ground with your legs out. Put your toes against a wall so your dog can't go around them. Start with your dog on your left side. Hold a treat in your right hand. Put the treat to your dog's nose so he can smell it, and move it across your legs. Hopefully he will step or jump over your legs to get the treat.

2. Kneel with your right leg outstretched, toes against the wall. Lure your dog with a treat and say an enthusiastic "hup!" to get him excited. He may be tempted to cross near your ankle as that is the lowest spot, so hold your treat closer to your thigh. When he crosses over your leg give him the treat.

3. Raise up on your back knee and try it again.

4. Kneel with your knee against the wall. If your dog tries to go under your leg, put a cushion there to prevent him.

WHAT TO EXPECT: This is usually a fun trick for dogs, and one that they enjoy performing. Practice when your dog is full of energy and he should get the hang of it within a week.

1. Put your legs out with your toes against the wall. With your dog on your left, and a treat in your right hand, lure him over your legs.

2. Kneel with your right leg outstretched. Hold a treat in your right hand, and lure your dog close to your thigh.

3. Raise up on your back knee and do it again.

4. Kneel with your knee against the wall. If your dog tries to go under your knee, use a cushion to prevent him.

Platform Jump

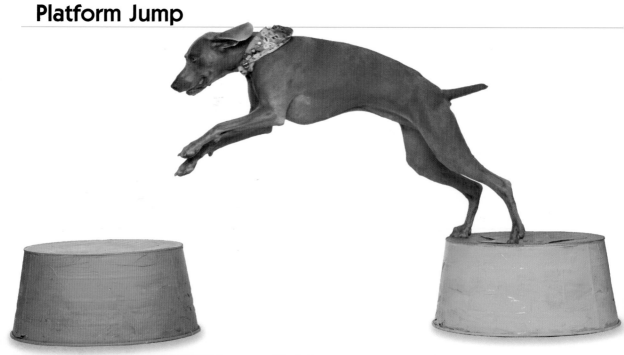

BEFORE YOU START

First teach your dog to put her **paws up** (page 60).

TROUBLESHOOTING

MY DOG STOPS HALFWAY, WITH TWO PAWS ON EACH PEDESTAL

That's fine; go ahead and give her the treat every time her front paws get on the second platform. Once you start separating them more she'll have to commit to the full jump.

TIP! Platforms should be sturdy with good traction. Your dog needs enough landing space; the farther apart the platforms, the larger they will need to be. Use two picnic benches (arranged end to end) for your platforms.

TEACH IT:

It takes courage to jump from one platform to another. Start small, and your dog will be leaping confidently in no time!

1 Set up two adjoining platforms. Use a treat to lure your dog onto the first platform (see **paws up**, page 60). Keep moving the treat to lure her onto the second platform.

2 Give her the treat when she reaches the second platform. Give her the treat while she is still standing on the second platform, and not after she's jumped off.

3 Gradually separate the platforms so that your dog is jumping farther distances. Say "hup!" and pat the second platform. Swing your hand to give your dog the idea to jump. Always give your dog a treat on the second platform.

4 If your dog jumps to the ground instead of the second platform, place a **duffle jump** (page 64) between the two platforms.

WHAT TO EXPECT: Increase the distance slowly, and only when you are sure your dog feels confident. Dogs often try to cheat and jump to the ground, so you will probably have to use the duffle jump at some point.

1 Set up two adjoining platforms. Use a treat to lure your dog to walk from one to the other.

2 Give her a treat while she is still standing on the second platform.

3 Gradually separate the platforms. Swing your hand to get your dog to jump.

4 If your dog jumps to the ground instead of the platform . . .

. . . place a duffle jump between the two platforms.

Double Balance Beam

BEFORE YOU START

First teach your dog to walk a **balance beam** (page 78).

TROUBLESHOOTING

MY LITTLE DOG WALKS ON JUST ONE SKINNY BEAM AND NOT BOTH

In the beginning the dog is still figuring out what works best, and trying different tactics. Just keep having her walk across, and after a while she'll figure it out on her own.

MY DOG JUMPS OFF IN THE MIDDLE

We really don't want your dog to get into this habit. Give your dog a steady stream of treats every second as she walks the beam. Hold the treats low, near the beam.

TIP! If your dog falls, don't end the session with her scared. Go back to something easy, like just putting her front paws on the beam, and end with that small success.

TEACH IT:

The balance beam trick is doubly impressive when your dog walks on *two* skinny beams! Two paws walk on each rail.

1. First teach your dog to walk a **balance beam** (page 78).

2. Replace the balance beam board with two 2 x 4–inch (50 x 100 mm) wood beams. Press the beams together so they look like a single board to your dog. Use a treat to lure her all the way across. Keep the treat low, near the beams.

3. Arrange the beams in a V shape, with the beams pressed together at the "start" end, and separated by 2 inches (5 cm) at the "finish" end. This V will force your dog to look down and think about where she is placing her feet.

4. Finally, make both beams parallel and separated so that they are shoulder width apart for your dog. Use a treat or your pointed finger to keep your dog going slow and straight. Can she do it?

WHAT TO EXPECT: This trick will take time, as your dog needs to learn the coordination to master it. Be patient with your dog. Work in baby steps and within a week your dog could be doing it.

1 Teach your dog to walk a **balance beam** (page 78).

2 Replace the board with two wood beams.

3 Set the beams in a V shape. The beams are touching at the start, and slightly separated at the finish.

4 Make both beams parallel. Use your pointed finger to keep your dog going slow and straight.

Build a double balance beam (page 116).

Build a Double Beam

SUPPLIES

- 4 cement bond beam blocks:
  8 x 8 x 16 inches
  (215 x 215 x 440 mm)

- 4 cement solid block caps:
  2 x 8 x 16 inches
  (50 x 215 x 440 mm)

- 2 wood 2 x 4–inch beams
  (50 x 100 mm)

- Cement glue (optional)

These standard building materials can be found at your home improvement store.

TIP! Check the wood for splinters. Sand them down or paint the boards.

BUILD IT:

Build a sturdy, safe double beam for your dog. Teach her how to walk on the **balance beam** with the instructions on page 114.

1. Set out your four cement bricks on a sturdy ground surface, with the grooves lining up. Push them snugly together.

2. Place one of your wood beams in the grooves. At this point you may have to adjust the placement of your bricks to get them the right distance apart.

3. This step is optional. The beams are pretty sturdy in the brick grooves, but if you want them to be even more sturdy and level, squirt some cement glue into the groove and squish your board down into it.

4. Place the caps on top of the bricks. Use cement glue if you wish.

FINISHING TOUCHES: If you want to make your double beam extra professional, add paint and skid tape for traction.

1 Set your four bricks with the grooves lining up.

2 Insert the beam in one set of grooves.

3 Optional: Add cement glue into the groove for additional stability. Squish the beam into it.

Teach your dog to walk across the double beam (page 114).

4 Place the caps on top of the bricks.

Trick it out with a coat of paint and some traction tape. Lookin' sharp!

Surfing

BEFORE YOU START
Try the **bobbing for popcorn** game (page 10) to increase your dog's water confidence.

TROUBLESHOOTING

MY DOG WON'T GO IN THE POOL, EVEN WHEN IT'S EMPTY
Some dogs are freaked out by the plastic surface. Put an inch (2.5 cm) of dirt or sand in the bottom of the pool. That should do the trick.

TIP! Swim trunks are not necessary for this trick. They're really not.

TEACH IT:
Standing on a body board is not easy. Teach your dog slowly until he gains confidence and masters this wobbly toy. Cowabunga!

1. At first your dog will be unsure about this new toy. Introduce him to the body board on dry land. Use a treat to lure him to step on it and let him nibble the treat while he has one or more paws on the board.

2. Put the body board in an empty wading pool. Again, use a treat to lure your dog to step on it and let him nibble the treat there.

3. Fill the wading pool with just a few inches (5 to 10 cm) of water and lure your dog with a treat just as you did before. Use your foot to stabilize the board.

4. Fill the pool with more water. Encourage your dog to jump onto the board and make a splash! If he's having fun, he'll be more confident.

WHAT TO EXPECT: Some dogs will be reluctant to get even their toes wet. Use extra-tempting treats like chicken, steak, or cheese to tempt your dog. Never force or lift your dog into the water, as that will make him even more fearful. It's better to take it slowly, even if it takes several sessions before your dog places his first paw in the water.

1. Your dog will be unsure about this new toy. Use a treat to get him to step on it.

2. Put the body board in an empty pool. Hold a treat to your dog's nose and slowly pull it forward to get him to step in the pool.

3. Add a few inches (5 to 10 cm) of water to the pool. Use your foot to stabilize the body board.

4. Fill the pool with more water. Act excited to give your dog enthusiasm to jump in!

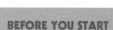

intermediate

Fetch a Ball

BEFORE YOU START

Go outside—dogs get more excited outside and are more likely to play fetch.

TROUBLESHOOTING

MY DOG WON'T CHASE THE BALL

Make the ball extra appealing by rubbing a treat all over the outside of it so it really smells.

MY DOG WON'T BRING THE BALL BACK

Never chase your dog when she is playing keep-away. Lure her back with a treat or run away from her to encourage her to chase you. Have a second ball, and pretend to be having lots of fun with the new ball.

TIP! Does your dog have a favorite ball or toy? Use that to play fetch. Trade her a treat for the toy when she brings it back to you.

TEACH IT:

A game of fetch provides hours of entertainment and exercise for you and your dog. (Probably mostly for your dog.)

1   Have an adult use a box cutter to make a 1½-inch (4 cm) slit in a tennis ball.

2   Squeeze the ball so the slit opens. Make sure your dog is watching as you drop treats inside.

3   Get your dog interested in the ball by bouncing it and batting it around. Toss the ball playfully away from your dog and encourage her to chase it. Try to get her to bring it back to you by patting your legs, acting excited, or running from her.

4   When your dog does (eventually) bring the ball back near you, squeeze it to let the treats drop out for her. As your dog is unable to get the treats out for herself, she will quickly learn to bring the ball back to you for her reward.

WHAT TO EXPECT: The hardest part of teaching this trick is getting your dog to bring the ball back the first time. Once she does it once, and gets the treat, it will go easier with each throw after that.

1 Cut a slit in a tennis ball.

2 Show your dog as you drop a treat inside the ball.

3 Get your dog interested in the ball by batting it around, and then toss it away from her.

4 Encourage your dog back to you. Squeeze open the tennis ball to let the treat out.

Flying Disc

TEACH IT:

Your dog will be flying high when you teach her to catch a disc!

1 Introduce your dog to this fun new toy by tossing it playfully or playing keep-away with it. Use your finger to spin the upside-down disc in circles.

2 When she seems interested, throw a "roller"—rolling the disc along its edge. Encourage your dog with "Get it! Get it!" and praise her excitedly when she does.

3 Encourage her to bring the disc back to you by clapping your hands and calling to her.

4 Trade her a treat for the disc.

5 Once your dog is eagerly chasing rollers, try throwing one in the air. Hold the disc with your fingers curled under the inside edge, and your index finger extended. When you throw it, use your wrist more than your arm and end with your finger pointing to where you want the disc to go.

6 Throw it away from your dog, and not at her. If she just watches it drop, go back to rollers for a while.

WHAT TO EXPECT: If at any point your dog loses interest in the disc, go back to the previous step. You may have to throw rollers for weeks before your dogs gets excited enough to catch one from the air.

BEFORE YOU START

Use discs specifically designed for a dog. Toy discs are too hard for a dog's teeth.

TROUBLESHOOTING

MY DOG HAS NO INTEREST IN THE DISC

Some dogs (often herding breeds) think chasing a disc is the funnest thing in the world. Other dogs don't. Use treats to get your dog to enjoy this game.

TIP! When learning to catch a disc, dogs often prefer softer rubber or canvas discs.

1. Spin the upside-down disc with your finger to get your dog interested in it.

2. When she shows interest, throw a roller.

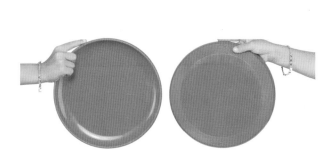

3. Clap your hands to your knees and call your dog to "bring it back."

4. Trade your dog a treat for the disc.

5. Curl your fingers under the inside edge. Use your index finger to point to where you want the disc to fly.

6. Hold the disc parallel and flick your wrist to throw it. Throw it away from your dog.

Coordination Ladder

BEFORE YOU START
You can use a regular ladder for this trick, or build a **coordination ladder** with the instructions on page 126.

TROUBLESHOOTING

MY DOG REFUSES TO WALK THROUGH THE LADDER

Turn the ladder upside down, which will make it just an inch (2.5 cm) tall. Put a leash on your dog and guide him through (but don't pull him).

MY DOG IS SO CLUMSY!

That's the purpose of this trick, to teach him coordination. He'll start to get better within a few days.

TIP! Have your dog practice walking over other things, like several brooms scattered on the ground. Can he figure out where to put his back feet?

TEACH IT:

Dogs pretty much don't know they have back feet—they lead with their head and everything else just follows. Ladder exercises develop your dog's back feet coordination.

1. Place your ladder alongside a wall to prevent your dog from walking off the side. Hold several treats in your hand. Get his interest and move your hand slowly forward. Keep your hand low so that your dog will still be able to see where he is walking while sniffing your treat.

2. After he has stepped through two or three rungs, give him one of the treats. Continue luring him forward with another treat.

3. Give your dog another treat when he gets to the end. Again, give the treat low, near the ladder.

4. Increase the pace as your dog gets comfortable. Move the ladder away from the wall. You may wish to put a leash on your dog at first, to help him stay on track.

WHAT TO EXPECT: At first, some dogs may not even like to stand still with their feet between the rungs. Give your dog time. If your dog is sidestepping, squirming, or jumping, walk slower as you take him though the ladder.

1 Hold a treat low, just above the rungs.

2 When your dog steps through a few rungs, give him a treat. Continue luring him forward.

3 Give another treat at the end. Keep your hand low, near the ladder.

4 Move the ladder away from the wall. Use a leash to keep your dog on track.

c'mon feets, stay in your own square!

Build a coordination ladder (page 120).

Build a Coordination Ladder

SUPPLIES
- PVC pipe (1 inch, 25 mm) length of approximately 22 feet (7 m)
- 4 PVC elbows (1 inch, 25 mm)
- 14 PVC T-joints (1 inch, 25 mm)
- PVC cutting tool or saw

Find PVC parts in the outdoor irrigation section of your hardware or gardening store.

TROUBLESHOOTING

SHOULD I USE GLUE?
PVC glue is not necessary; just knock the joints together on the ground a few times to get them good and tight.

TIP! Lay all your pieces in place on the ground first, just like in the photo. That way you can double-check your plan.

BUILD IT:

Build a coordination ladder for your dog to run through. Teach her how to use it with the instructions on page 124.

1 Cut your PVC pipe. You will need:

8 side pieces (13 inches [33 cm] each)
4 half-side pieces (5.35 inches [13.5 cm] each)
4 spacer pieces (2 inches [5 cm] each)
6 rung pieces (16 inches [40 cm] each)
6 leg pieces (7 inches [18 cm] each)

2 Cutting PVC pipe takes a bit of muscle. Use a hand saw or a special PVC cutting tool.

3 Assemble the ladder boxes, working on one box at a time. Attach the elbows at the four corners. When the ladder is on the ground, the elbows should point up toward the sky.

4 Insert the legs and you're done!

FINISHING TOUCHES: The length of the legs will determine how high your ladder will be. Short-legged dogs, older dogs, and puppies may need a lower height. You can also remove the legs for smaller dogs, or during initial training.

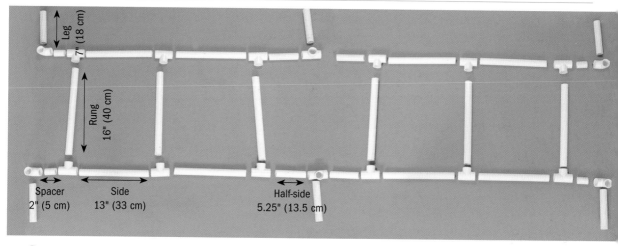

Leg 7" (18 cm)

Rung 16" (40 cm)

Spacer 2" (5 cm) Side 13" (33 cm) Half-side 5.25" (13.5 cm)

1 Cut your PVC pipe pieces. Lay the ladder out as shown.

2 A PVC cutting tool will give you a nice, clean edge.

3 Assemble the ladder boxes. Attach the four elbows to the corners.

4 Finish by inserting your six leg pieces.

Teach your dog to use the coordination ladder (page 124).

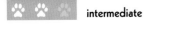

Figure-8's Through My Legs

BEFORE YOU START

Start with the **peekaboo** trick (page 58) first, so your dog gets used to going through your legs. Practice figure-8's on your own before involving your dog.

TROUBLESHOOTING

MY DOG IS TOO BIG TO FIT THROUGH MY LEGS

Whoops! Looks like you need to grow longer legs!

MY DOG NIPS MY FINGERS

Hold your hand cupped with a treat between your fingers, near your palm. That way your dog noses your palm and not your little fingers.

TIPS!

1. Hold several treats in each hand.
2. Move slowly.
3. Give a treat each time your dog is at the side of your leg.

TEACH IT:

Zigzag, zigzag, your dog runs in and out and between your legs making a figure eight. Now that's teamwork!

1. Hold several small treats in each of your hands. Start with your dog at your left side and hold a treat to her nose. Move the treat forward, and between your legs.
2. Have your hands meet in the middle. Get her to follow the new hand to pull her through your legs.
3. Give her a treat at the side of your leg.
4. Lure her back through your legs.
5. Have your hands meet in the middle, and your dog now follows your new hand.
6. Guide her out to your left side, and you did it! Give her a treat by your left leg.

WHAT TO EXPECT: Most dogs can learn this trick in a few days. Some dogs can be a little apprehensive about going through your legs at first (especially little dogs). Keep practicing and you'll have an impressive trick!

1 Have your dog at your left. Move the treat forward and between your legs.

2 Your hands meet in the middle. Your dog follows your new hand through your legs.

3 Give her a treat at the side of your leg.

4 Back through your legs.

5 Hands meet in the middle and your dog follows your new hand.

6 And she comes out on your left side again!

Rolling Hoop Dive

BEFORE YOU START

First teach your dog to **hoop jump** (page 84).

TROUBLESHOOTING

MY DOG KNOCKS THE HOOP OVER

It will help if your dog runs through perpendicularly. So if your dog starts on your left, roll the hoop more to your right.

MY DOG IS SCARED

Roll the hoop slowly, and start it rolling off to the side of your dog (see question above).

TIP! Always roll the hoop away from your dog, and not toward her. She will want to chase it if it's running away!

TEACH IT:

This high-energy trick is a great workout for your dog. You roll hoops across the yard and your dog chases them down and dives through their centers!

1. Hold a large hoop in front of you and have your **dog hoop** jump (page 84). Give her a treat for each jump.

2. Walk forward holding the hoop in front of you low to the ground, to accustom your dog to jumping through a moving object. Give her a treat for jumping through it.

3. As you walk forward, send the hoop rolling in front of you a short distance and use an excited tone to tell her to "get it!" Your dog may run to the hoop, and run back to you, not understanding. Keep alternating between walking with the hoop and sending it rolling. This is the hardest step of learning, so keep up the enthusiasm!

4. This next step is training for you! Practice throwing a hoop fast and straight by balancing it on your collarbone as you grip the bottom underhanded. Let it roll down and off your wrist.

WHAT TO EXPECT: Dogs with a strong prey drive will love this trick. It can take a while to teach, so stick with each step until your dog is doing it well. Don't forget the treats!

1 Hold a hoop in front of your stomach and have your dog jump through it.

2 Hold the hoop low as you walk. Have your dog practice jumping through a moving hoop.

3 Roll the hoop a short distance as you walk and send your dog to "get it!"

4 Balance the hoop on your collarbone. Hold it underhanded. Roll the hoop down your arm and off your wrist.

Jump Through My Circled Arms

BEFORE YOU START

First teach your dog to **hoop jump** (page 84).

TROUBLESHOOTING

MY DOG IS TOO BIG TO FIT THROUGH MY ARMS

Widen your arms to allow space between your hands, or hold a rope between your hands.

MY DOG JUMPS THROUGH THE HOOP, BUT WON'T JUMP THROUGH MY ARMS

Some dogs are nervous about jumping close to your arms and head. Alternate between the hoop and arm circles.

TEACH IT:

After your dog has mastered jumping through a hoop, get rid of the hoop and have her jump through your arms. Now that's a cool trick!

1. Warm up with a few **hoop jumps** (page 84). Use the arm that is farthest from your dog to hold the bottom of the hoop. This will cause your head to lean away from your dog, rather than into your dog.

2. Gradually widen your arms around the hoop as your dog continues her jumps. Be careful to keep your head out of the way.

3. Use a smaller hoop and wrap your arms around it. You can make your large hoop smaller by disconnecting the ends, cutting off a section, and reconnecting it.

4. Continuing in the same session, set aside the hoop and cue your dog to jump through your arms. A larger dog may require your hands to be disconnected. If your dog resists, go back to using the hoop.

WHAT TO EXPECT: Dogs often take two steps forward and one step back with this trick. They may jump through your arms on the first day, but may require you to pick up the hoop the next day for a refresher.

1 Warm up with a few hoop jumps. The arm farthest from the dog holds the bottom of the hoop.

2 Widen your arms around the hoop.

3 Use a smaller hoop. Wrap your arms around it.

4 Continuing in the same session, try one jump through the small hoop and the next jump with no hoop at all.

Roll Over

BEFORE YOU START
Work on a soft surface, like carpet or grass. (Your dog won't want to roll over on a hard floor.)

TROUBLESHOOTING

MY DOG STANDS UP
Two things will help: move your hand very slowly, and keep your hand low to the ground.

MY DOG FLOPS ONTO HIS SIDE, BUT WON'T FINISH THE ROLL
First of all, the side flop is already a success; that's pretty good. For now, just ask him to do that much and give him the treat. Don't push him the rest of the way over with your hand—that could scare him and make him not want to do it at all anymore.

TIP! It helps if you teach this on a bit of a slope (like a small hill in your backyard). It's easier for your dog to roll downhill.

TEACH IT:

This one is a standard that every trick dog should know. Your dog rolls onto his back and all the way over onto his stomach again.

1. With your dog lying down, hold a yummy treat in front of his nose.

2. Tell your dog to "roll over" and move the treat slowly from his nose to his shoulder. His nose will follow the treat, and he will shift onto one hip—that's great! Give him a treat right now to reward him for this baby step.

3. Let's see if we can get him to roll more. Keep moving your treat slowly from his shoulder toward his backbone. He will roll onto his back, trying to reach the treat.

4. A little more . . . and he did it! Give him the treat right away, and tell him what a great job he did!

WHAT TO EXPECT: Dogs can be squirmy when learning this trick, so it's important to be calm and move very slowly. Try both sides, as dogs usually like to roll in one direction more than the other.

1. Hold a treat in front of your dog's nose.

2. Slowly move it toward his shoulder. Your dog will shift onto one hip.

3. Keep moving the treat toward his backbone.

4. He did it!

Skateboard

BEFORE YOU START
It will be helpful to first teach your dog to put her **paws up** (page 60).

TROUBLESHOOTING

MY DOG RUNS AFTER THE SKATEBOARD BUT DOESN'T STEP ON IT
This is common in the beginning, as your dog is still a little afraid of the skateboard. Keep practicing step #1 to get her used to stepping on this unstable object.

TIP! Make an extra large skateboard by attaching casters to the bottom of a body board or kick board.

TEACH IT:

Some dogs (often bull breeds and terriers) go crazy for skateboards. Try it with your dog and see if she's a natural boarder!

1. Start with the skateboard on carpet or grass where it's quieter and moves slower. Use a treat to lure her to put her front paws on it. Hold the board steady with your foot.

2. Take it outside and encourage your dog to investigate it and see how it works. It's not so scary, is it? Roll the skateboard back and forth in front of your dog. If she moves toward it, roll it *away* from her so it runs away like a prey animal. Did she chase it? Praise her excitedly when she catches it, especially if she steps on it!

3. Skate on the skateboard yourself. When she sees it moving she'll get more excited about it. She may try to chase it and step on it.

4. Run and toss the skateboard ahead of you and chase it yourself. Use your voice to get your dog excited and chasing it, too!

WHAT TO EXPECT: Some dogs have a natural drive to chase the skateboard and jump on top of it and sometimes bite it. Few dogs love the skateboard on their first try, and most take several weeks of play to get excited about it.

1. Start on carpet or grass. Hold the board with your foot and use treats to get your dog to step on it.

2. Take it outside and let your dog investigate it and see how it works. Roll it away from your dog. Does she chase it?

3. Skate on it yourself. Seeing it move will make it more exciting. Your dog may try to chase it and step on it.

4. Toss the skateboard rolling in front of you and chase it yourself. Your dog will want to get it before you do and may jump on it.

Handstand

BEFORE YOU START
Add traction to a board by gluing carpet to it.

TROUBLESHOOTING

I CAN'T GET MY DOG TO STEP ON THE BOARD AT ALL
The hardest part of this trick is step #1. It's going to be tricky to keep moving your treat in such a way to get your dog to back up onto the board. Keep experimenting and you'll get there.

TIP! Feeling frustrated? Tell your dog you know she's doing the best she can. That will make both of you feel better.

WHAT TO EXPECT: Not all dogs are built the same way, and some will be able to climb a higher board than others—that's okay. This trick will take a few weeks to teach to your dog.

TEACH IT:

"My dog can sit." "My dog can shake hands." "Yeah, well my dog can do a handstand!"

1   Put your board on the ground. Hold a treat in your fist at your dog's nose height. As she sniffs and nibbles it, push it slowly toward her nose. Keep pushing it toward her and she'll take a step back. Watch closely. The second her back foot touches the board, say "good!" and release the treat.

2   Raise the board slightly and try the same thing again. Push the treat toward your dog's nose to cause her to take more steps backward. As long as she keeps her back feet on the board, keep giving her treats every few seconds.

3   Raise the board higher. Put your hand low to the ground to keep her nose in the right position.

4   Lean the board against the wall to make it even higher. Your hand will now have to be almost at the floor.

1 Push the treat slowly toward your dog's nose to get her to back up. When her back foot touches the board, say "good!" and release the treat.

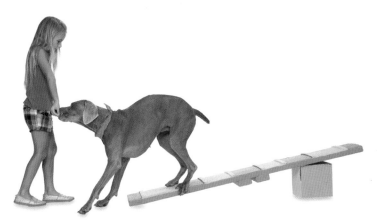

2 Raise the board a little. Keep pushing the treat toward her to get her to take additional steps backward. Give her treats every few seconds as long as her feet remain on the board.

3 Raise the board. Put your hand low in order to make it comfortable for your dog.

4 Lean the board against the wall. As your dog's back feet climb higher, lower your hand to the floor.

advanced

Teeter-Totter

BEFORE YOU START
First teach your dog to walk a **balance beam** (page 78).

TROUBLESHOOTING

MY DOG IS SCARED TO GO PAST THE MIDDLE OF THE TEETER-TOTTER
As he gets close to the middle, keep setting treats on the board, just an inch (2.5 cm) out of his reach.

MY DOG JUMPS OFF THE MIDDLE OF THE TEETER-TOTTER
This happens when you move too fast. Hold your treat lower, close to the board, and move it slowly so your dog's nose stays right by your hand. Give him a treat after every few steps so he doesn't have to wait until the end. You can also place the teeter-totter alongside a wall, so he can't jump off that side.

TIP! The "bang" sound is scary for some dogs. With your dog off-leash, show him how the teeter-totter moves and let it bang quietly a few times.

TEACH IT:

Dogs who compete in the sport of agility learn to run across a teeter-totter. Your dog can learn it, too!

1. **Build a simple teeter totter** using the instructions on page 142. Set a box under each end of your teeter-totter. Hold a treat in front of your dog's nose, and guide him to step onto the board.

2. Slowly move your treat across the board to guide your dog. Hold the treat low so that your dog can still see the board while sniffing the treat. Give him the treat at the end (while he is still standing on the board and not after he has jumped off).

3. Remove the box at the starting end of the teeter-totter. This will make a bigger drop when your dog crosses the middle of the board.

4. Move slowly as you get to the middle of the board, when it is just about to fall.

5. Once your dog is crossing easily, remove the last box. If your dog is having problems, go back a step for a while.

WHAT TO EXPECT: Some dogs are more confident learning this trick than others. The most important thing is not to let your dog have a fearful experience. It's better to go slowly and let him go at his own pace than to rush him in to the full-height teeter-totter too quickly.

1 Put boxes under both ends of the board. Use a treat to lure your dog up.

2 Slowly guide him to walk across the board. Keep your hand low.

3 Remove the first box. This will make a higher drop.

4 Go slowly near the middle of the board, when it is about to drop.

5 Remove the last box. Now your dog is crossing the teeter-totter for real!

Build a simple teeter-totter (page 142).

Build a Teeter-Totter

SUPPLIES

- PVC pipe (1¼ inch, 32 mm)
- 4 PVC elbows (1¼ inch, 32 mm)
- 4 PVC T-joints (1¼ inch, 32 mm)
- Board (8 x 1 feet x 1 inch)
  (2.5 m x 300 x 22 mm)
- Two wood blocks (2 x 2 x 12 inches)
  (500 x 500 x 300 mm)
- Turf or carpet for traction
  (8 x 2 feet, 2.5 m x 600 mm)
- Wood glue
- PVC cutting tool or saw
- Screws and screwdriver
- Staple gun

Find PVC parts in the outdoor irrigation section of your hardware or gardening store.

BUILD IT:

Build a simple teeter-totter for your dog. The board rests on the base, making it easy to dismantle for travel or storage.

BUILD THE BASE

1. **Assemble the base.** Cut the PVC pipe with a PVC cutting tool or a saw. Assemble the pieces together as shown. Knock it on the ground a few times to get it good and tight.

2. **Assemble the stanchion.** The length of the uprights will determine the height of your teeter-totter. Shorter uprights will be easier for your dog while he is learning.

3. Fit the stanchion into the base.

BUILD THE BOARD

4. Glue your two wood blocks parallel, in the center of your board. Leave enough space between them to fit one of your PVC T-joints.

5. For added strength, put some screws through the board and into the wood blocks.

6. The board is slippery for a dog. Add traction by attaching outdoor turf or carpet to your board using a staple gun or small brads.

FINISHING TOUCHES: Lay the board on top of the base, with the wood beams straddling the base crossbar.

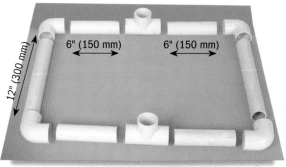

1 Assemble the base.

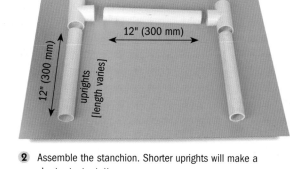

2 Assemble the stanchion. Shorter uprights will make a shorter teeter-totter.

3 Fit the stanchion into the base.

4 Glue the wood beams to the board. Space them so a T-joint fits between them.

5 Put in several screws. Screw first into the board and down into the block.

Teach your dog to run across the teeter-totter (page 140).

6 Use a staple gun or small brads to secure the carpet.

Volleyball

TEACH IT:

This trick is totally not hard to teach. Toss a ball in the air and your dog will bop it back to you with his nose! Spike!

1. Get your dog excited to play with a plush toy; toss it around and squeak the squeaker. Don't push it toward your dog, but rather skitter it away from him to get him to chase it.

2. When your dog is focused on the toy, toss it in the air in a slow arc toward him. When he catches it, say "good!" and give him a treat.

3. While your dog is still feeling playful, switch to a lightweight inflatable ball (a real volleyball is too heavy for a dog). Toss the ball in a high arc so it comes down above your dog's nose. Your dog will jump up and try to catch the ball, but because it is so big it will just bounce off his nose and back to you!

WHAT TO EXPECT: This trick is easier to teach than it looks! Once your dog is able to catch a toy, he could be bouncing a ball off his nose on his first day. If your dog is scared of the ball, use a balloon instead as it falls much slower (take the balloon away from your dog when you are done because you don't want him swallowing any balloon pieces).

1. Make the toy skitter away from your dog so he will chase it.

2. Toss it in a slow arc toward your dog. Say "good!" when he catches it.

3. When your dog tries to catch a ball, it will bounce off his nose.

Sit Up

TEACH IT:

Sitting up improves your dog's balance and builds her core strength. Plus, it's really cute.

1. Start with your dog sitting. Stand directly behind her, with your heels together and your toes pointed apart. Hold a treat in front of her nose to keep her attention.

2. Use your treat to slowly guide her head back and straight up, until she lifts her front paws. Steady her chest with your other hand. Let her nibble treats while sitting up in this position.

3. Keep practicing. As your dog improves, use a lighter touch on her back and chest.

WHAT TO EXPECT: Some dogs will be able to do this trick easily, while others (often larger dogs) may have a much harder time finding their balance. If your dog is jumping at the treat, move it more slowly. If your dog stands up on her hind legs, keep your hand lower and say "sit." Hold the treat at her face height.

1. Stand behind your dog with your feet in a V shape. Hold a treat to her nose.

2. Move the treat up and back. Steady her chest with your other hand.

3. Over time, use a lighter touch as your dog finds her balance.

Fit Ball

BEFORE YOU START

It will help if your dog already knows **paws up** (page 60).

TROUBLESHOOTING

MY DOG WON'T PUT HER BACK FEET ON THE BALL

This is an athletic trick, and it is harder for some dog body types than others. It's still good exercise for her to balance with two feet on the ball.

TIP! Keep your older or injured dog in control and moving slowly when interacting with the ball.

TEACH IT:

Improve your dog's balance, strength, and coordination by having her balance on top of a wobbly fit ball. Can she do it?

1. Use a large cardboard box or bucket to stabilize your fit ball. Move a treat from your dog's nose over the ball to get her to put her paws up. Let her nibble treats in your hand to keep her there. Gently rock the ball back and forth so she uses her rear legs to balance.

2. Move the treat just out of your dog's reach to coax her to climb on top of the ball. She will try to move around the ball. Keep moving your body so the ball is between you and your dog.

3. Give your dog treats as long as she is trying, even if she can't quite get on top of the ball. If she does get on the ball, let her nibble treats from your hand and lean against your hand for balance.

4. Once your dog is feeling comfortable, walk slowly around the ball so she has to stand up to follow your treats.

WHAT TO EXPECT: Once dogs realize that they get treats for interacting with the fit ball, they often bounce on it happily!

1 Move a treat over the ball to get your dog to bring her front paws on it.

2 Move the treat out of your dog's reach. Your dog will try to circle the ball. Keep moving so that you stay opposite her.

3 If your dog makes it on top of the ball, let her nibble treats from your hand. She may need to lean against your hand for balance.

4 Walk slowly around the ball to get your dog to move her feet and stay balanced.

Magic Trick

BEFORE YOU START
First teach your dog to **fetch a ball** (page 120).

TROUBLESHOOTING

MY DOG GETS EXCITED AND BRINGS BACK THE FIRST BALL SHE SEES
Don't touch the ball she brought back (if it's not correct). Send her back to the balls over and over until she gets the right one. Then give her a treat.

TIP! Use a strong-smelling treat inside the ball, like a big chuck of steak, or liver treats.

TEACH IT:

Amaze your friends as your dog answers life's toughest questions: "Who is the greatest kid to ever live?" "Should I have to clean my room?" and "Is it my sister's fault?" Behold, your dog knows the answer!

1. Gather a few identical tennis balls. Have an adult cut a slit in each one with a box cutter. When you squish the ball, you'll be able to drop a treat inside.

2. On each ball, write a different answer to a question (such as "yes," "no," "maybe," your name, your dog's name, and numbers).

3. Ask a question: "Am I the greatest magician ever?" Send your dog to the balls to select the answer.

4. (Secret: Before you start, put a treat in the ball that you want your dog to pick.)

5. Give your dog a treat every time she brings back the correct, treat-filled ball.

WHAT TO EXPECT: If your dog already knows how to fetch, she can pick up this trick pretty quickly.

STEPS:

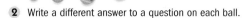

1 Cut a slit in each tennis ball. When you squish the ball, you can drop a treat inside.

2 Write a different answer to a question on each ball.

3 Ask your dog a question and send her to the balls to select the correct answer.

4 (Secret: Your dog will select the ball that has the treat in it!)

5 Give your dog a treat every time she brings back the correct ball.

They call me "Jadie the Great!"

Biscuit Under the Sofa

TROUBLESHOOTING

MY DOG STANDS THERE AND DOESN'T EVEN TRY

Let her have a few easy successes by pushing the treat just a few inches (5 to 10 cm) under the sofa and letting her get it with her paws. The next time, push it just out of her reach.

TIP! Large, crunchy dog biscuits work well as they crumble out from the ribbon.

TEACH IT:

How smart is your dog? This logic test challenges her to figure out how to get a dog biscuit out from under the sofa. Sound easy? You might be surprised!

1   Tie a long ribbon around a dog biscuit. Show your dog as you push the biscuit about 18 inches (45 cm) under the sofa.

2   Your dog will try various tactics to get the biscuit, such as sticking her nose under the sofa and pawing under the sofa.

3   After 20 seconds show your dog as you pull the ribbon to reveal the biscuit. Don't let her have the biscuit yet. Repeat this again by pushing the biscuit under the sofa, letting your dog try to get it for 20 seconds, and then pulling it out yourself to show her how to do it.

4   On the third repetition wait for your dog to figure out how to pull the ribbon herself. You may have to point at the ribbon or wiggle it to help her get the idea.

5   When she does pull it out, untie the biscuit from the ribbon and let her eat it. Smart dog!

WHAT TO EXPECT: It may take your dog a few tries to figure out how to pull the ribbon, but once she does, she will enjoy pulling biscuits out from under all sorts of places!

1 Tie a ribbon around a dog biscuit and push it under the sofa.

2 Let your dog try on her own to get the biscuit.

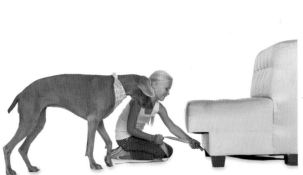

3 Show her how to do it; pull the ribbon to expose the biscuit.

4 On the third time, see if your dog has learned to use the ribbon on her own.

5 Smart dog! Untie the biscuit and give it to her.

Shell Game

BEFORE YOU START

Clay flowerpots work best for this trick as they are heavy and have a hole in their base.

TROUBLESHOOTING

IS MY DOG SUPPOSED TO SMELL WHERE THE TREAT IS OR REMEMBER WHERE IT IS?

She smells it. To your audience, it looks like she is remembering.

MY DOG BARELY SNIFFS IT

Some dogs are very gentle and only lightly sniff the pot. You have to be a good trainer and learn to read your dog. A light sniff is her way of telling you where the treat is.

MY DOG KNOCKS EVERYTHING OVER

Some dogs are pushy and knock everything over. Use a less tasty treat like a dog kibble. She'll be less excited about that.

TIP! All dogs have very good noses, but breeds with long noses (like the Weimaraner in the photo) have exceptional smelling ability.

TEACH IT:

Hide a treat under a pot. Shuffle several pots around and see if your dog can show you where the treat is hiding.

1 Flowerpots have a small hole in the bottom to let the water drain out. Tape a treat inside the pot right up against that hole, so that your dog will be able to easily smell it through the hole.

2 Show your dog as you place a treat on the floor and then cover it with the flowerpot.

3 Say "find it!" Try to get her interested in the flowerpot. Tap the hole on tope or quickly lift it and put it back down to show her that a treat is hiding underneath.

4 When she sniffs or paws the flowerpot at all, say "good!" and lift the pot, allowing her to get the treat.

5 Add two more pots. You may have to hold them down so that your dog doesn't knock them over. If she paws at an incorrect pot do not lift it, but encourage her to "keep looking."

6 When your dog shows a lot of interest in the correct pot, say "good!" and lift it.

WHAT TO EXPECT: The shell game game can be confusing for your dog at first, so be gentle with her and avoid saying "no." As your dog improves you can stop taping the treat to the pot—she'll be able to smell the one hiding underneath.

1 Tape a treat against the hole in the flowerpot.

2 Show your dog as you place a treat on the floor and cover it with the flowerpot.

3 Say "find it!" Try to get her interested in the flowerpot by tapping it or lifting it.

4 When she sniffs or paws the flowerpot, say "good!" and let her get the treat.

5 Add two more pots. You may have to hold them down so that your dog doesn't knock them over.

6 When your dog shows a lot of interest in the correct pot, say "good!" and lift it.

Pull up the Fishing Rope

TEACH IT:

Tie a treat to the end of a rope, and toss it over the balcony. Can your dog figure out how to pull up the rope to get the treat? If she doesn't pull far enough, the rope (and treat) will slip back down!

1. Attach a treat to the end of a thick, knotted rope. Show your dog the treat and then hang the rope a foot or two (30–60 cm) over the edge.

2. Your dog may bite or scratch at the rope. Reward each of her attempts by pulling the rope a few inches (5 to 10 cm) closer to her.

3. After she has pawed and pulled the rope a few times, you should have pulled it inch by inch to the top. Give her the treat. (It's important to give her the treat from the rope and not a different treat from your pocket.)

4. Once your dog gets the hang of it, let her pull up the rope all by herself. Eventually she will figure out how to bite the rope and walk backwards to pull it up.

WHAT TO EXPECT: Don't worry if your dog is not getting it at first . . . allow her time to figure it out on her own. Logic games challenge your dog to experiment with different ways to accomplish a goal, which increases their intelligence.

BEFORE YOU START

Play the **biscuit under the sofa** game first (page 150) to teach your dog to pull a rope.

TROUBLESHOOTING

MY DOG JUST STARES AT THE ROPE

If the treat is too far away, your dog won't know how to get it. Drop the treat just 6 inches (15 cm) over the edge and let her reach over to grab it. Next time put it an inch (2.5 cm) farther.

TIP! Do this trick on a balcony or staircase. Drop the rope through the railing bars.

1 Tie a treat to the end of the rope and hang it a few feet over the edge.

2 Every time your dog bites or paws at the rope, pull it up a little as a reward.

3 When it gets to the top, give her the treat.

4 Eventually your dog will bite the rope and walk backwards to bring the treat to the top.

Dog Silhouette

SUPPLIES
- Canvas
- Tape
- Paint (high-gloss acrylic paint is recommended)
- Paintbrushes

TROUBLESHOOTING

I DON'T KNOW HOW TO TILE A PHOTO ONTO SEVERAL PIECES OF PAPER

Take your photo to a photocopy store. They can print a large-size black-and-white copy for under $4.

TIP! If you mess up, use white paint to fix your mistake.

MAKE IT:

If you can trace, then you can do this art project. Outline a silhouette of your dog and paint around it.

1. Take a photo of your dog (profile shots work best). On your computer, crop it close around the dog. Resize it to the size of your canvas and print it. For a large canvas, the photo will tile onto several pages, which can be taped together.

2. Cut out around your dog's silhouette.

3. Lay your photo on the canvas. Use painter's tape to hold it in place. Trace around the edge of the photo with a pencil. Don't worry if your pencil goes haywire . . . everything outside of the dog photo will be covered in paint anyway.

4. Now you have an outline of your dog.

5. Paint the area outside of the outline. Use a large paintbrush for the edges, and a tiny brush for the area closest to the pencil line.

6. Voilà! A masterpiece!

FINISHING TOUCHES: Use a different color paint to add details like a collar, bandana, or hair ribbon.

1 Print a photo of your dog. Large photos will tile onto several pieces of paper.

2 Cut out your dog.

3 Tape your photo to the canvas and trace around it with a pencil.

4 Now you have an outline of your dog.

5 Paint the area outside of your outline.

6 Your masterpiece is finished!

Wooden Nameplate

SUPPLIES

- Wooden board or plaque
- Paint and tiny paintbrush, or paint pen
- Tape
- Ribbon
- 2 eye hooks

TROUBLESHOOTING

I DIDN'T PRESS HARD ENOUGH, AND NOW I CAN'T SEE THE INDENTS

Can you see the indents a little bit? If so, cut your paper right up to the edge of the letters on all four sides. That way it will be easy to line it up to your existing indents, and you can trace over it a second time.

TIP! If you are right-handed, paint the left edges of each letter first. Then turn the plaque upside down and paint the rest.

MAKE IT:

Define your dog's space with a personalized nameplate. Hang it above his bed or over his food bowl.

1. Paint a base color on your wooden plaque.

2. Using your computer, print out your dog's name in a font that suits him.

3. Tape the printout to your plaque so it doesn't move. Use a pen to outline the letters. Press hard with the pen.

4. Remove the paper, and you'll see your letters indented in the wood. Pretty neat!

5. Use a tiny paintbrush or a paint pen to fill in the letters.

6. Attach eye hooks to the top, and hang it with a ribbon. How cool is that!

FINISHING TOUCHES: Add stickers, stars, glass beads, or other embellishments around the edges.

1 Paint a base color on your wood plaque.

2 Print your dog's name in a fun font.

3 Use a pen to outline the letters. Press hard.

4 Your pen will leave an indent in the wood.

5 Fill in the letters using a paintbrush or paint pen.

6 Attach eye hooks and ribbon to hang it.

Shoelace Bead Collar

MAKE IT:

Your special dog deserves a special collar. Choose your own colors to make this unique beaded collar. It's functional and strong.

1. Fold your shoelace in half. String the loop through the buckle and then through the D-ring.

2. The plastic tips of shoelaces are called aglets. Pull the aglets up through the loop and pull tight.

3. String the other two laces the same way.

4. String two beads onto each set of laces. Both aglets won't fit through the bead at once, so push one aglet through at a time.

5. String a different colored bead onto laces 2 & 3 and laces 4 & 5. Keep repeating this pattern. Periodically tighten everything by pushing all the beads toward the buckle. Measure it against your dog's current collar to know when the length is right.

6. Turn the collar upside down, so the D-ring is touching the table. String the ends through the other part of the buckle.

7. Put the ends of one set of laces back through itself. Repeat for each set of laces.

8. On the first set of laces, bring one end up around each side and tie in a knot. Repeat for each set. The knot should be snug, but not so tight that it squeezes the collar width.

9. Add hot glue to cover the knots.

10. After the glue has dried, trim the ends. Beautiful!

FINISHING TOUCHES: Can you think of a different design? How about a rainbow? Or half the collar in one color and half in another color? Try different patterns with your beads, or string a special bead in the center. Have fun with it!

SUPPLIES

- 3 oval shoelaces. Length should be double your dog's neck size, plus an additional 20 inches (50 cm).
- ¾" (2 cm) buckle
- ¾" (2 cm) D-ring
- Pony beads
- Hot glue gun

TIP! The collars shown here use 45" (114 cm) laces.

STEPS:

1 String the loop through the buckle and then through the D-ring.

2 Pull the aglets up through the loop and pull tight.

3 String two more laces.

4 String two beads onto each set of laces.

5 String a bead onto laces 2 & 3 and 4 & 5. Repeat the pattern for the length of your dog's collar.

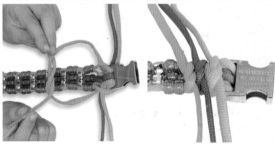

6 Flip the collar so the D-ring is touching the table. String the ends through the buckle.

7 Put the ends of each set of laces back through itself.

8 Bring one end around each side and tie in a knot. The knot is on the underside of the collar.

9 Cover the area with hot glue.

10 Trim the ends. Beautiful!

Personalized Dog Bowl

SUPPLIES
- Tape
- Pencil
- Transfer paper
- Paint pen

TROUBLESHOOTING

OH NO, I MESSED UP THE PAINT!
Dip a cotton swab in soapy water and use it to erase the paint smudges. Act quick, because once the paint has dried it will be permanent.

TIP! Press the paint pen onto paper a few times before you start, to get the paint flowing smoothly.

MAKE IT:

Customize your dog's dinner bowl using this cool pointillism technique.

1. Print your dog's name from your printer. Fonts with serifs (the little thingies on the ends of the letters) work well. Cut out the name and tape it to the back (non-ink side) of a sheet of transfer paper.

2. Cut a rectangle around the name and transfer paper. Cut between each letter, starting at the bottom of the letter. Don't cut completely to the top; leave the very top still attached.

3. Tape the letters onto the bowl. Because the bowl is wider at the bottom than the top, you'll have to spread the letters a little at the bottom (which is why we cut slits in the previous step).

4. Use a pen or pencil to trace the outline of each letter.

5. Remove the paper and you will see the outline of your letters from the transfer paper. Use a paint pen to follow the outline by making small dots with a paint pen.

FINISHING TOUCHES: Let the paint dry for a day, and then wash the bowl with soap and warm water to remove the marks left from the transfer paper.

1 Print your dog's name. Cut it out and tape it to the non-ink side of a sheet of transfer paper.

2 Cut between each letter. Leave the very top still attached.

3 Tape the letters to the bowl. You'll have to spread the letters at the bottom because the bowl is wider at the bottom.

4 Trace the outline of each letter.

5 You now have an outline of the letters on the bowl. Use a paint pen to make dots.

Washer Collar Tag

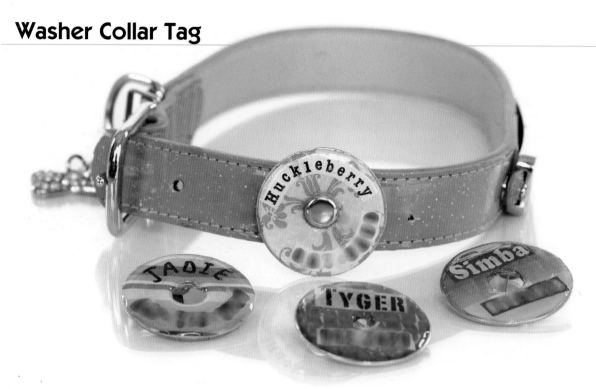

SUPPLIES

- Washer with a small hole
- Pretty paper
- Glue
- Clear nail polish or a dimensional finish product such as Judikins Diamond Glaze or Mod Podge Dimensional Magic
- A brad

TIP! Make a matching washer as a necklace or zipper pull for yourself.

MAKE IT:

Give your dog's collar extra pizazz with this custom collar tag. Use it as his ID or just as decoration. It's easy and inexpensive to make.

1. Trace around your washer onto scrapbook paper, wrapping paper, or any other kind of pretty paper.

2. Cut out your circle. You don't need to cut out the small hole in the middle.

3. Smear a little glue onto the washer, making sure to get full coverage. Drop the paper circle onto it and slide it into place. Use a pen to poke out the hole in the middle.

4. Decorate your collar tag with your dog's name, stickers, letters cut out of a magazine, or whatever you wish.

5. Top the finished design with a protective coat of clear nail polish or a dimensional finish glaze.

6. Attach it to your dog's collar by putting a brad through one of the existing holes on the collar.

FINISHING TOUCHES: The ends of the brad on the inside of your dog's collar may annoy him. Use a bit of duct tape to secure them down.

1 Trace around your washer onto scrapbook paper.

2 Cut out your circle.

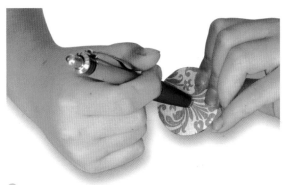

3 Glue the paper to the washer. Use a pen to poke out the center hole.

4 Write your dog's name or other decoration on the paper.

5 Finish with clear nail polish or dimensional finish.

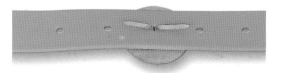

6 Use a brad to attach it to a hole in your dog's collar.

Dog Hair Artwork

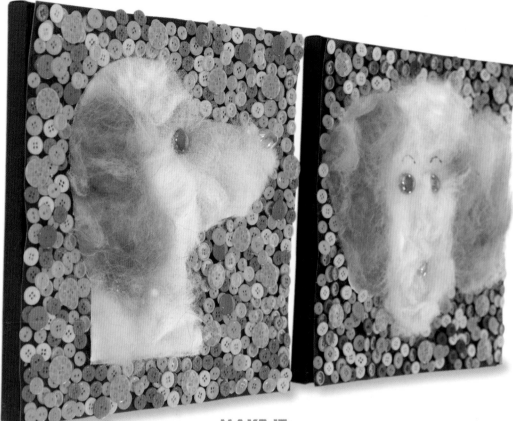

MAKE IT:

Does your dog shed? A lot? Then this is the craft for you!

1. Use a thick marker to draw a picture of your dog onto a sheet of paper. Include the outline of his ears and any spots that he has.

2. Spread glue inside the outline. Press chunks of fur into the glue (try not to let your finger touch the glue or things will get sticky!). Don't worry if fur goes outside the outline, we'll cut that part off in the next step. After the glue has dried, a little hairspray will set it.

3. Turn the paper over. You should be able to see your marker outline through the paper. Cut out the outline. This will give your fur a nice, sharp edge.

4. Glue the fur head to a canvas of a contrasting color. Add embellishments like glass beads for his eyes and nose, a ribbon in his hair, or a collar around his neck. Use puffy paint to outline the ears or draw in eyebrows.

5. Put a dot of glue on each button and stick it to your canvas.

FINISHING TOUCHES: Set your work with a little more hairspray. Let it dry for a full day before you hang it or your buttons may slide down the paper.

SUPPLIES
- Dog hair
- Canvas or sturdy paper
- Buttons
- Glass beads or embellishments
- Glue
- Hairspray

TIP! Collect fur from your dog's brush every time you groom him.

1 Draw an outline of your dog. Include his ears and any spots that he may have.

2 Drizzle glue inside the outline and press chunks of fur onto the glue.

3 Turn the paper over and cut out the outline.

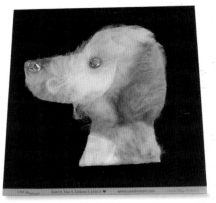

4 Glue to a canvas. Add embellishments for the eyes, nose, and collar.

5 Put a drop of glue on each button and add it to the canvas.

intermediate

Dog Rides in a Wagon

BEFORE YOU START

It will be helpful if you first teach your dog to put her **paws up** (page 60).

TROUBLESHOOTING

MY DOG WON'T GET IN THE WAGON

Make sure the wagon wheel is secure and won't move. Put a doormat in the wagon to give your dog traction. Put a cement brick next to the wagon as a step to help her get in.

MY DOG KEEPS JUMPING OUT

She is a little scared. Let her jump out if she needs to, but try to keep her in by feeding her treats.

TEACH IT:

Pull your dog around the neighborhood in a wagon. What a buddy!

1. Wrap a towel around the wagon wheel to keep it from moving. Hold several small treats in your hand and lure your dog to put her **paws up** into the wagon (see page 60 for tips).

2. Once her front paws are in the wagon, let her have one of the treats.

3. Continue moving your hand forward to encourage her to put her back feet up. When she is all the way in the wagon, give her another treat.

4. Keep giving her treats every few seconds to encourage her to stay in the wagon, as she will probably want to jump out.

5. Back up one step while holding your hand in front of her and telling her to "stay." Go back and give her another treat.

WHAT TO EXPECT: This trick will go a little slower than you think. Make the wagon a "happy place" where your dog gets a lot of treats. Once you start pulling the wagon, do so very slowly and give treats often.

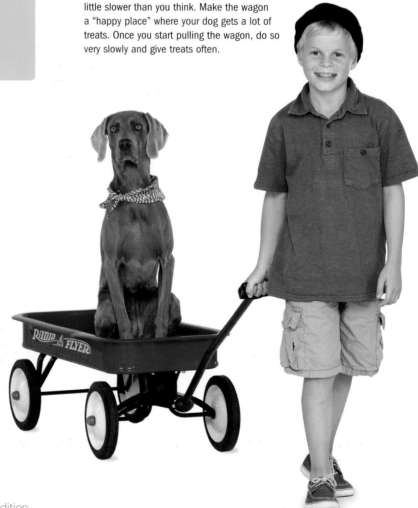

1 Wrap a towel around the wheel. Use a treat to lure your dog to put her paws in the wagon.

2 Keep moving the treat forward to encourage her to lift her back feet into the wagon.

3 Keep moving the treat forward to encourage her to lift her back feet up.

4 Keep giving her treats every few seconds so that the wagon is a happy place.

5 Tell her to "stay" and back up a step.

Turn on a Tap Light

BEFORE YOU START
First teach your dog to put his **paws up** (page 60).

TIP! Keep your eye on your dog's feet. Give him the treat as soon as his foot touches the object.

TEACH IT:

It's getting dark—can you turn on the light? Send your helpful dog to step on a tap light.

1. First, teach your dog to put his **paws up** on a stool or chair (page 60). Move a treat from his nose to above the stool to get him to step up on the stool. Give him the treat when he is up.

2. Next, do a paws up on a shorter stool. Use a stool that is sturdy and won't tip over.

3. Do a paws up on a cement brick. Next, securely tape your tap light to the brick. Use a treat to lure your dog to step onto the brick. When he does, say "good!" and give him the treat. If he happens to step on the tap light itself, give him three treats and excited praise!

4. Now tape the tap light to a smaller object, such as an upside-down dog bowl. Say "lights!" and use a treat to try to get him to step on it. Give him a treat if he touches the tap light at all (even if it doesn't actually turn on).

5. Finally, tape the tap light directly to the floor. (Your dog may try to scratch at it, which is why we need to tape it.) Say "lights!" and see if he can step on it. If he has trouble, go back to the previous step.

WHAT TO EXPECT: You're going to be tempted to skip a few steps in this trick but it's best not to. Increase difficulty slowly by doing a paws up on just a slightly smaller object each time. Stay on each step for one day.

1 First, practice doing paws up on a stool.

2 Do a paws up on a shorter stool. Reward your dog every time he steps onto it.

3 Tape the tap light to a cement brick and try another paws up.

4 Tape the light to an upside-down dog bowl. Give your dog a treat for touching it with his paw.

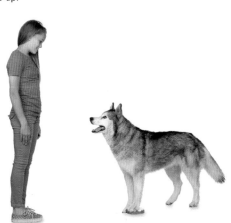

5 Tape the light to the floor. Can your dog do a paws up on it now?

Close the Door

BEFORE YOU START

First, teach your dog to **touch a target stick** (page 76).

TROUBLESHOOTING

MY DOG WON'T TOUCH THE TARGET STICK OR THE TAPE

Put a dab of peanut butter on it. The instant he touches it (or licks it) say "good!" and give him a treat.

TIP! Use a regular door for larger dogs, and a kitchen cabinet for small dogs.

TEACH IT:

Here's another useful trick—teach your dog to push the door closed with his nose.

1. First teach your dog to **touch a target stick** (page 76). Practice having him nose-touch your wooden spoon near the door. Keep moving the spoon closer and closer to the door. Give him a treat each time.

2. Hold the spoon right up against the door and get him to touch it. Then tape the spoon to the door and see if he'll touch it. You may have to put your finger on it or tap it to draw his attention to it. When he does, say "good!" and give him a treat.

3. Remove the target stick but keep a big piece of tape in the same spot. Say "close the door" and tap the tape to try to get your dog to nose-touch it. Awesome! Give him a big treat.

4. Open the door a little and ask him to "close the door." If he doesn't nose-touch it hard enough on the first try, tell him to do it again. If he starts to get discouraged, go back to giving him a treat for even a tiny nose-touch.

WHAT TO EXPECT: If your dog knows how to touch a target stick, then he will pick up this trick pretty easily. It's important to say the word "good!" at the exact instant that your dog's nose touches the target. Don't forget to give a treat every time.

1 Practice having your dog touch a target stick near the door.

2 Tape the target stick to the door. Point at it or tap it to get your dog to touch it.

3 Remove the target stick but leave the tape.

4 Open the door and tell him to "close the door." If he doesn't push hard enough, send him back to do it a second time.

Shake Hands

BEFORE YOU START

Test whether your dog is **right-pawed or left-pawed** (page 88). That's the paw he will use to shake hands.

TROUBLESHOOTING

MY DOG DOESN'T EVER LIFT HIS PAW

Dogs will mimic your body language. If you are holding the treat in your right hand, lean to your left. Your dog will lean in the same direction, making it easier to lift his paw. You can also try tapping the back of his paw to give him the idea to lift it. Be quick when he lifts it, and say "good!" and give him the treat.

TIP! Dogs don't like their paws touched. Don't hold on to your dog's paw; let him pull it away whenever he wants.

Dogs shake hands like this!

TEACH IT:

Every polite pooch needs to learn to shake hands!

1   Hold a treat in your fist, low to the ground. Encourage your dog to paw at it by saying "get it!" Your dog will try to poke his nose into your fist—just move your hand away a little to discourage this.

2   Eventually he will get frustrated and paw at your hand. He will only do this once, so be ready for it. The instant that his paw lifts off the ground (whether or not he actually touches you), say "good!" and open your hand to let him have the treat. If he is nosing your hand at the same time that he lifts his paw, that's fine, say "good!" and give him the treat.

3   Once your dog has the hang of this, raise your hand higher and say "shake." Eventually, do it without any treat in your hand.

4   After your dog shakes your hand, give him a treat from your other hand. It's best to give him the treat while his paw is still in your hand.

WHAT TO EXPECT: Some breeds are more pawsy than others, but any dog can learn this cute trick. Practice a couple of times per day and always end on a high note. Within two weeks your dog could be politely shaking hands.

1. Hold a treat in your fist low to the ground and encourage your dog to "get it!"

2. He will eventually paw at your hand. Say "good!" and open your hand.

3. Raise your hand higher. Keep the treat in your pocket this time.

4. Try to give your dog the treat while his paw is still resting in your hand.

High-5

BEFORE YOU START
First teach your dog to **shake hands** (page 174).

TIP! Depending on your dog's body shape, he may not be able to reach above his shoulder. Crouch down to make your hand lower.

TEACH IT:
Gimme five! (Or . . . actually, gimme four!)

1 Say "shake" and have your dog **shake hands** (page 174). Give him a treat with your other hand.

2 Say "high-five, shake" and hold your hand with your fingers pointing toward the sky. Your dog won't be able to rest his paw in your hand this time, so it will be more like he is scratching your palm. Say "good!" at the exact moment he touches your hand. Give him a treat, of course.

WHAT TO EXPECT: With a solid shake, your dog can learn to do a high-five within a few training sessions.

1 Have your dog shake your hand.

2 Say "high-five, shake" and hold your hand with your fingers up. Give your dog a treat.

Sit Before Chowtime

TEACH IT:

It's never too early to start learning manners. Teach your polite puppy to sit before receiving his dinner.

1 First teach your dog to **sit** (page 187). When it is mealtime, prepare your dog's bowl and hold it out of his reach. Tell him to "sit." He may be so excited that he temporarily forgets the meaning of the word, so give him several chances to sit. Help him to sit by lifting the food bowl a little over his head and moving it toward him, which can cause his head to look up and his rear to drop, especially if his back is against a wall.

2 If he does not sit, turn away and put the bowl out of his reach. Come back in one minute and try again.

3 Try again a minute later. When your dog does finally sit, even for a second, say "good!" and immediately put his bowl down as a reward for his politeness.

WHAT TO EXPECT: Don't be too strict with your dog, as the goal is not that he do a perfect sit, but rather that he build a habit of asking politely for his dinner.

BEFORE YOU START
Before you teach this trick, first teach your dog to **sit** (page 187).

TROUBLESHOOTING

MY DOG JUST WON'T SIT
It's not fair to ask your dog to sit before chowtime if he hasn't been taught to sit in the first place. Does he really understand the word "sit"?

TIP! Don't "free feed" your dog. Offer him a meal and if he hasn't finished it in fifteen minutes, pick up the bowl.

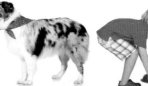

1 Tell your dog to "sit." Give him a few chances to remember what this word means.

2 If he doesn't sit, take the bowl away.

3 When your dog does sit, say "good!" and set down his bowl.

Say Your Prayers

BEFORE YOU START

First teach your dog to put her **paws up** (page 60).

TROUBLESHOOTING

MY DOG DROPS ONE PAW OFF THE STOOL WHEN I GIVE HER THE TREAT FROM MY LOWER HAND

She is having a hard time reaching the treat. Hold the treat closer to her paws instead of her chest. Hold the treat in the center and not more toward one leg.

TIP! It really helps to have several small treats in each hand, so you can keep your dog's focus the whole time.

TEACH IT:

In this trick your dog bows her head between her paws like she is saying her prayers. Aww, what a good doggy!

1. Stand to the side of your dog. Hold several small treats in both hands. Hold one treat out to your dog's nose.
2. Say "paws up" and move the treat forward and up over the stool.
3. Let your dog nibble the treat from that hand.
4. Say "prayers." Reach your other hand up from below, and slowly bring both of your hands together until they touch near your dog's front paws. Take away your first hand and try to get your dog to nibble treats from your lower hand.

WHAT TO EXPECT: There is going to be a bit of squirming at first, but hang in there.

1. Hold several small treats in both hands. Hold one to your dog's nose.

2. Move the treat forward and up to get your dog to put her paws up on the stool.

3. Let your dog nibble the treat in that position for a few seconds.

4. Reach your other hand up from below, and give her a treat from that hand.

Tidy Up Toys into Toy Box

BEFORE YOU START
First teach your dog to **fetch** a ball (page 120).

TROUBLESHOOTING

MY DOG WON'T EVEN FETCH THE TOY
Your dog will be more interested in a yummy-smelling toy—make one by stuffing treats inside a tube sock and tying it in a knot.

MY DOG WON'T BRING THE TOY BACK
Your dog likes his toy. You need to have a treat in your hand that's even *better* than the toy! Break out the chicken, ham, steak, lunch meat, or cheese.

MY DOG DROPS THE TOY BEFORE GETTING TO THE TOY BOX
Your dog is confused. Work with him for a while on just **fetch** (page 120). He'll be back on track in no time!

TIP! If your dog has a favorite toy, use that one to teach him.

TEACH IT:

Does your dog leave his toys all around the house? Teach him to put his toys away in his toy box. Now that's a useful trick!

1   Get your dog excited by squiggling his toy around on the floor; pretend it is a small animal that is running away from him.

2   When your dog is excited, toss his toy.

3   Encourage him back by showing him a treat. As he comes closer, move the treat toward the back of the toy box.

4   When your dog opens his mouth to get the treat, his toy will fall into the toy box! Yay!

5   Sometimes the toy will fall near the toy box, but not quite in it. That's okay; your dog needs time to learn, so give him the treat anyway.

6   After about 100 practices, your dog will be able to do it on his own. Then he can help you pick up *your* toys, too!

WHAT TO EXPECT: This is a hard trick, and your dog is going to need a lot of help from you to learn it. Be encouraging and never tell your dog that he did it wrong (or else he won't want to try at all anymore!).

1 Get your dog excited to play with a toy.

2 Toss the toy.

3 Encourage him back with a treat. Move the treat to the back of the toy box.

4 When he opens his mouth to get the treat, the toy will fall into the toy box!

Make a toy box for your dog (page 182).

5 If the toy doesn't quite make it in, that's still okay.

6 Practice 100 times and your dog will have it down!

Make a Doggy Toy Box

SUPPLIES
- Cardboard box
- Fabric
- Glue
- Duct tape
- Ribbon

TIP! For a professional look, iron your fabric before you glue it to your box.

MAKE IT:

Does your dog have a lot of toys? Make him his very own box to store them in.

1 Start with any size cardboard box. Cut a piece of fabric the same width as the width of your box, and long enough so that it will wrap from one side of the box all the way to the other side (plus a little extra, which will fold inside the box rim).

2 Use glue or spray adhesive to stick the fabric to the box. The ends will fold into the inside of the box.

3 Cut another piece of fabric the width of the other side of your box. Again, cut it a little longer so that it wraps inside the rim of the box.

4 Glue the second strip of fabric to the box, keeping it stretched tight as you glue. Use your hands to smooth out any wrinkles.

5 Use a strip of colored duct tape along each edge to cover up the seams and give it a polished finish.

6 Glue a ribbon around the top rim.

FINISHING TOUCHES: Personalize your dog's toy box by gluing craft foam letters onto it. Neat!

1 Cut fabric the width of your box.

2 Glue the fabric to the box.

3 Cut a second strip of fabric the width of the other side of your box.

4 Glue the fabric, smoothing it tight with your hands.

5 Use a strip of colored duct tape along each edge.

Teach your dog to put his toys into his toy box (page 180).

6 Glue a ribbon along the top rim.

Hide Your Eyes

BEFORE YOU START
Not all dogs like having their face touched, so ask your parents if it's okay to do so.

TROUBLESHOOTING

MY DOG JUST SITS THERE WITH TAPE ON HIS NOSE
Yeah, some dogs do that. Try sticking the tape different places: the top of his head, above or below his eye. Tap the tape a little to point it out to your dog. Encourage him by saying "get it!"

TIP! It's important to react fast with this trick. Have the treat ready in your hand, so you can pop it into his mouth the instant he swats the tape.

TEACH IT:

"Are you shy? Are you covering your eyes?" How cute is that?!

1. This trick is easiest if your dog is sitting or lying down, but if he changes position don't worry about it. Stick a piece of tape to his muzzle. Tap it a bit to draw his attention to it, and tell him "cover!"

2. Your dog will try to remove the tape by swatting at it—perfect! At the exact moment that his paw touches his face, say "good!"

3. Immediately after you say "good," pop a treat in his mouth. (Timing is everything . . . you have to react fast!)

WHAT TO EXPECT: Most dogs will swat at the tape pretty readily. Remember to give a treat EVERY time he swats at the tape. After several weeks of practice, try it one time without the tape. Just tap your dog's muzzle at the place where the tape was, and say "cover." If he doesn't cover his eyes, go back to using the tape for a while.

1 Stick a piece of tape on your dog's muzzle and tell him to "cover!"

2 He will use his paw to swat it off. Say "good!" at that exact instant.

3 Quickly follow up with a treat.

Come

TROUBLESHOOTING

MY DOG RUNS OFF!
Do not chase your dog, as that will only encourage him to play keep-away. Act interested in something on the ground, or toss a toy around and act like you're having fun with that. That should pique your dog's curiosity and get him to come to you.

TIP! Always reward your dog for coming to you, whether it be with praise, a treat, or a play session.

TEACH IT:

Does your dog come to you when you call him? Teach him how.

1 Most dogs like excitement and will eagerly come to you when you act exciting. Say "come," smile, and pat your legs.

2 When your dog comes to you, have a party! Give him a treat and tell him how wonderful he is. That's exciting, right?

3 Try it at different times of the day, in different places. When it's dinner time, call "come" and have his dinner bowl ready.

WHAT TO EXPECT: Only call your dog to "come" for good things (like treats or play) and never for bad things (like taking a bath or getting scolded). That way every time he hears "come," your dog will think, "Oh boy! I'm going to come as fast as I can!"

1 Pat your legs and call "come."

2 Give your dog a treat and tell him how great he is!

3 Call your dog to "come" for his dinner.

Sit

TEACH IT:

Every dog should know how to sit. All dogs can learn this trick, even young puppies.

1 Stand in front of your dog and hold a treat to his nose. Say "sit" and slowly move the treat up and back over your dog's head. This should cause his nose to point up and his rear to drop.

2 The instant his rear touches the floor say "good!" and give him the treat.

WHAT TO EXPECT: Move slowly, don't talk, and don't make a lot of extra movements. This will allow your dog to focus on your treat. Most dogs start to learn this trick within a few days, although it will take about 100 repetitions before they can do it consistently.

> **TROUBLESHOOTING**
>
> **MY DOG JUMPS UP AT THE TREAT**
> Hold the treat lower, so that he can reach it while standing.

> **TIP!** If your dog is squirmy and not sitting, try working in front of a wall so your dog won't have room to back up.

1 Move a treat from his nose, up and back toward his tail.

2 This should cause his rear to drop. Say "good!" and release the treat.

Down

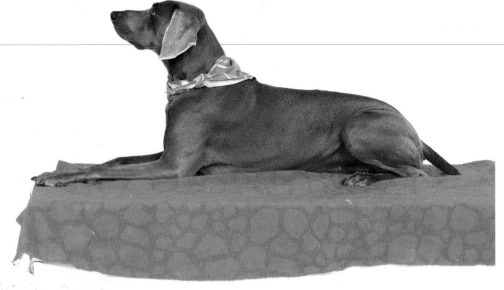

TROUBLESHOOTING

WHEN I SLIDE THE TREAT AWAY FROM MY DOG, SHE STANDS UP

Instead of sliding it away, try holding it between her paws for a while. She'll get tired of hunching over and will eventually lie down. You can also position your dog in front of a wall, so she can't back up away from you.

MY DOG PAWS AT MY HAND

Ignore it and just keep working with her. Don't tell her "no." Wear gloves to protect you from scratches.

TIP! Teach this trick on carpet or grass. (Dogs don't like to lie down on hard floors).

TEACH IT:

Teach your dog to lie down. This comes in handy when you need your dog to settle and be still, or stay in one place.

1. Start with your dog sitting. Hold a treat to her nose to get her attention.

2. Tell her "down." Lower the treat down, between her paws. She will hunch her head down to the floor. If she stands up, it may be that you put the treat too far in front of her paws.

3. Very slowly slide the treat away from her. She will probably lie down. As soon as she lies down, open your hand and let her have the treat. Give her the treat on the floor, while she is still lying down.

WHAT TO EXPECT: When dogs are first learning this trick they may stand up, back up, or paw at your hand. It may take a few days of practice. Don't get frustrated—just try again.

1. Hold a treat to her nose to get her attention.
2. Move the treat down, between her paws.
3. Slowly slide the treat away from her, toward you.

Stay

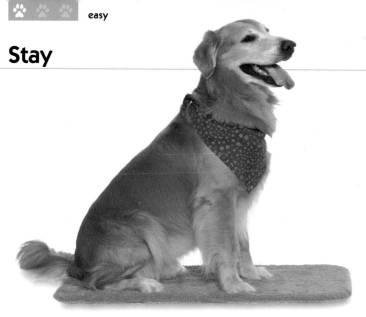

TROUBLESHOOTING

MY DOG KEEPS GETTING UP
Act very calm. Use slow and deliberate movements.

MY DOG STANDS UP A SECOND BEFORE I GIVE HIM THE TREAT
Don't get the treat out of your pocket until you are standing in front of him, as the treat will pull him forward.

TIP! It will be easier to teach this trick indoors, where there are fewer distractions.

TEACH IT:

Sometimes you need your dog to stay still.

1. Start with your dog sitting. Stand directly in front of him and put your palm in front of his nose. Say "stay" in a firm tone (but not loud or mean).

2. Keep your hand up as you take one step backward. Look directly into your dog's eyes to hold him in place.

3. Wait one second, then step forward. Say "good stay" and give your dog a treat with your other hand (keep your first hand up until he has the treat). Only give the treat while your dog is sitting. If he stands up at the last second, do not give him the treat (or else he will think he earned the treat for standing up!).

WHAT TO EXPECT: Gradually increase the time you ask your dog to stay, as well as the distance between you. You want your dog to be successful, so if he is standing up, go back a step.

1. Say "stay" and hold up your hand.

2. Take one step backward, keeping your hand up and keeping eye contact.

3. Step forward and reward your dog.

ACKNOWLEDGMENTS

ACKNOWLEDGMENTS

CHILD MODELS—Thanks to our brave, funny, crazy kids: **Asa Carman** 5, **Jackson Duke** 9, **Taylor Duke** 12, **Adrianna Hahn** 6, **Kylie Horn** 11, **Sofia Merritt**, 7, **Aiden Meyndert** 9, **Madelyn Meyndert** 8, **Mackenzie Mueller** 5, **Claire Peter** 7, **Joseph Ruano** 9, **Noah Ruano** 7, **Savannah Shingler** 6, **Daisy Worthington** 7, **Noah Worthington** 9.

DOG MODELS—Thanks to our beautiful, talented, and incredibly patient dogs: **Jadie** (Weimaraner), **Huckleberry** (Portuguese Podengo), **Duke** (Vizsla), **Sage** (Siberian Husky), **Caesar** (Standard Poodle), **Tank** (Golden Retriever), **Anki** (Japanese Akita), **Chris** (Australian Shepherd), **Lassie** (Rough Collie), **Laci** (Dalmatian), **Bonny** (Shih Tzu), **Owen** (Golden Retriever), **Iris** (Terrier mix), **Skippy** (Jack Russell Terrier).

Thanks to dog wranglers **Claire Doré** and **Joel Norton**, kid wrangler and dog petter **Heidi Horn**, craft consultant **Ciegi Shaw**, and **Mimi Green** dog collars.

PHOTOGRAPHER: CHRISTIAN ARIAS

"I've shot several of Kyra's dog books over the years and our shoots are always a lot of fun (and a little crazy!) . . . dogs wrestling in the green room, dogs upside down on the couches, dogs sneaking into the lunchroom for a snack (yum!). Because our shoots weren't crazy enough, Kyra decided to add kids this time . . . (so we had dogs and kids wrestling and rolling upside down!). It was a lot of fun for me to shoot, especially since I'm expecting my first child!"

—Christian Arias & Jade, Slickforce Studios, www.slickforce.com

Photo ©Sean Cummings

ALSO BY KYRA SUNDANCE

AWARD WINNING BOOKS AND DVDS!

Want more ways to have fun with your dog? Kyra Sundance's books and DVDs are beloved worldwide for their enthusiastic approach to teaching your dog. Her straightforward step-by-step methods are accompanied by clear photos and video to make dog training a snap! Kyra's positive reinforcement methods instill a cooperative spirit in your dog and develop in them a love of learning.

EARN YOUR DOG'S TRICK TITLE!

Teach 15 tricks to your dog and demonstrate them to any witness. Have your witness sign your application form and mail it in, and your dog will receive his Novice Trick Dog title and official certificate. Teach more tricks to earn his advanced titles. You can do it! domorewithyourdog.com

DoMoreWithYourDog.com

ABOUT THE AUTHOR

Kyra
(Can almost do a back handspring by herself if someone is spotting her)

Jadie
(Can't spell very well but is only 5 and is still learning)

Hi. I'm Kyra. Here's some stuff about me . . . I like to wear cowboy boots and clomp around loudly. I can almost do a back handspring. I can make traffic lights turn green by staring at them real hard. Scorpions glow in the dark. (That one's not really about me, but I thought it was kinda neat.)

Here's some stuff about Jadie . . . She likes ham. She can't spell very well (which is why I'm typing). She takes pink snuggy bear with her everywhere she goes. She is five. She can ride a skateboard. She really likes ham. (She wanted me to write that again.)

KYRA SUNDANCE is a world-acclaimed stunt dog show performer, celebrity dog trainer, and internationally best-selling author.

Kyra authored seven dog training books. *101 Dog Tricks* has sold over a half-million copies in 18 languages and is one of the top dog training books of all time.

Kyra and her Weimaraners have starred in shows for the king of Morocco in Marrakech, in Disney's *Underdog* stage show in Hollywood, and in circuses and professional sports halftime shows. They have performed on *The Tonight Show, Ellen, Animal Planet,* and had their own television series called *Showdog Moms & Dads.*

Kyra is nationally ranked in competitive dog sports and is a set trainer for movie dogs. As a lecturer on positive training methods, her enthusiasm inspires audiences to develop fun and rewarding relationships with their own dogs. In her spare time she enjoys ultrarunning and hanging out with her dogs and her husband, Randy, on their ranch in California's Mojave desert.

Do More With Your Dog!

DoMoreWithYourDog.com